THE CEO SPEAKS

THE CEO SPEAKS

THE ESSENTIAL LAWS OF BUSINESS AND SUCCESS

RUDY NASH

RUPA

Published by
Rupa Publications India Pvt. Ltd 2024
7/16, Ansari Road, Daryaganj
New Delhi 110002

Sales centres:
Bengaluru Chennai
Hyderabad Jaipur Kathmandu
Kolkata Mumbai Prayagraj

Copyright © Rupa Publications India Pvt. Ltd 2024

The views and opinions expressed in this book are the author's own and the facts are as reported by him which have been verified to the extent possible, and the publishers are not in any way liable for the same.

All rights reserved.
No part of this publication may be reproduced, transmitted, or stored in a retrieval system, in any form or by any means, electronic, mechanical, photocopying, recording or otherwise, without the prior permission of the publisher.

P-ISBN: 978-93-6156-080-4
E-ISBN: 978-93-6156-280-8

First impression 2024

10 9 8 7 6 5 4 3 2 1

The moral right of the author has been asserted.

Printed in India

This book is sold subject to the condition that it shall not, by way of trade or otherwise, be lent, resold, hired out, or otherwise circulated, without the publisher's prior consent, in any form of binding or cover other than that in which it is published.

Contents

1. The New Chief Executive Officer Takes Over — 1
2. But Wait, Let's Listen to the Departing CEO — 14
3. With Greater Power, Comes Greater Responsibility — 27
4. Employee is Distressed! What Should a CEO Do? — 38
5. Playing Favourites? No, Strictly No — 47
6. Hey CEO, What's Your Leadership Style? — 60
7. Making Sense of the CEO's Management Style — 68
8. From Good to Great CEO — 84
9. Go, Get It: The CEO Who Motivates — 100
10. See Inside, CEO: Finding Your Authentic Self — 110
11. The Differences Between the Best CEOs and the Average Ones — 124
12. Chief Executive Officer Thoughts: What Great Leaders Do First and Best — 137
13. The Compassionate CEO: How to Hold Your Team Accountable with Empathy — 156
14. The Post-Pandemic CEO — 163
15. What's Your Style? Finding the Right Balance — 169
16. What do the Employees Need? Being a CEO in Times of Uncertainty — 175

17. Staying Strong: The CEO's Guide to Resilience
    and Adaptability   180
18. Looking Ahead: The Future CEO's Path to
    Leadership   187

1

The New Chief Executive Officer Takes Over

Despite the fact that it takes longer than you anticipate, patience pays off in unexpected ways.

New chief executive officers (CEO) are regularly confronted with a dilemma. In public, the people around them have great expectations for what they can do, but at the same time, in secret, those same people have doubts about their abilities. Consequently, many newly appointed chief executive officers fail to recognize the amount of effort required to establish confidence in their leadership, which is an essential component of their capacity to effectively drive change. They rush forward with daring new projects before acquiring the complete support and trust of all stakeholders, which leads them into difficulty. They are buoyed by outward gestures of support and ready to make their mark, therefore they are eager to make their mark.

New chief executive officers are not to blame for falling into the speed trap. When all is said and done, the prevalent notion is that they have approximately 90 days to demonstrate their worth to their respective organizations. In reality, however, the procedure takes significantly more time than that, as indicated by both our research and our personal experience. In the end, it was discovered that it takes a full two years to win the confidence of all of the stakeholders. The only way for chief executive officers to truly set the circumstances for long-term success is for them to concentrate on creating trust from a strategic and intentional standpoint during that period.

Where did we get the number that was based on two years? In this century, approximately 1,400 CEOs who have headed companies that are included in the S&P 500 have been thoroughly studied. The first thing needed was a reliable method of identifying and assessing confidence in them. In most cases, we consider confidence to be a trait that possesses a social value, since it enables leaders to exert influence over other people. On the other hand, it also has a monetary value: investors assign multiples to stocks that indicate their trust in the continued potential of enterprises to create shareholder returns. As a result of our reasoning, we concluded that the enterprise multiple may be regarded as a measurable proxy for the confidence that CEOs develop in their leadership style across the various stages of their tenure in office. The enterprise multiple is calculated by dividing the total enterprise value of a firm by its profits before interest, taxes, depreciation and amortisation (EBITDA). The higher the enterprise multiple, the more confidence there is in a CEO's capacity to provide superior performance in the future.

Once we had devised a metric that was applicable to a wide range of situations, we turned back the past to examine how the CEOs who participated in our research had been able to win people's confidence year after year. Spencer Stuart, a leadership-advisory firm that consistently partners with organizations to improve CEO performance (and that employs Claudius and Jason), was the source of the interview data that we coupled with the insights that we gathered from those interviews. The growth of revenue, total shareholder returns, profitability and environmental, social and governance (ESG) performance were some of the other criteria that we considered when evaluating the effectiveness of the CEO. With the use of this combination of quantitative and qualitative data, we were able to obtain substantial evidence on the rate at which leaders acquire the support of stakeholders over time, the strategies they employ to deal with the difficulty and the advantages that result from everything being done correctly.

When new CEOs focus strategically on confidence building during their first two years, they set off a virtuous cycle that leads to a remarkable and consistent increase in their companies' enterprise multiples in the years that follow. This led us to a striking discovery: although it typically takes much longer than we think for new CEOs to get others to believe in them, when they do this, they set off a cycle that leads to a remarkable increase in the enterprise multiples of their companies. Increases like this are referred to as the confidence premium.

Little to no premium is created over the first two years of a CEO's term in their position. During that time period, the words and actions of a new CEO are closely scrutinized; nonetheless, it is typically too early for anyone to adequately analyse the repercussions of such actions. Nevertheless, beginning in the third year, things begin to alter. The gap between the two groups continues to increase, eventually reaching a difference of roughly four points. CEOs who started out with comparable multiples progressively begin to be perceived as greater or lower performers, and from that point on, the gap between the two groups continues to widen. When one analyses the impact of such a multiplier on, for example, the $30 billion median market valuation of an organization that is part of the S&P 500, the confidence premium amounts to close to $10 billion. This may sound like a modest amount, but it is quite significant. A significant lesson may be learned from this situation: if you are a new CEO and you want to maximize the value you will create over the long term, you will need to earn the confidence of all stakeholders through patience and systematic approach during your first two years in executive leadership. In this chapter, we will provide direction on how to accomplish that precisely by drawing not only on the findings of our research and analysis but also on looking at a professional who has just joined a big company as its chief executive officer.

A great track record is one of the few things that may create confidence more than anything else, but if you are a new CEO, you also begin with a clean slate. So what should we do next? We have developed a list of five essential procedures that you ought to implement in a strategic manner.

Create a Slow and Steady Pace

This is very important. We've dealt with a lot of new CEOs who, feeling the pressure to achieve early successes, hit the ground running. They initiate a variety of programmes and chase various goals without securing the alignment of the board, their leadership team or other important stakeholder groups. This is something that we've seen happen quite a bit. Due to the fact that the race they are competing in is not a sprint but rather a marathon, it goes without saying that this strategy is unsuccessful. Running a marathon takes patience, endurance and a strategy that can be maintained over the long run. When it comes to a marathon, time is on your side. If you want to go fast, you have to go slow. Your ability to maintain your efforts and assist others in developing faith in your leadership will be facilitated by your acceptance of that idea and your ability to pace yourself suitably.

Imagine a professional who is a new CEO of a major firm and finds himself caught in the speed trap he has created for himself. All of his stakeholders were made aware of the fact that they were at the very beginning of a marathon, which allowed him to release himself from the restraints of time constraints. After spending 20 years with the company and following in the footsteps of previous CEOs who had only been with the company for a short period of time, he came to the realization that his new organization was highly unstable, lacked a long-term strategic view and had a culture that did not reflect the ideals that it had stated. At the outset, he made it very apparent to the board of directors, the family that owned the company and the company itself that he wanted to serve in the job for a period of 10 years. He assured them that those years would be the most successful that the organization had ever experienced.

Following that, he was tasked with re-establishing the culture. He and his leadership team gave their new programmes catchy titles, such as the 'Best 10 Strategy' and the '3Fs' (which stands for 'fearless, founder, family'), and they discussed them on a frequent basis. He and his team started celebrating small victories in performance and rewarding long-tenured executives with new leadership positions once the employees started to understand that they had a CEO who planned to stay around, provide stability and bring back the company's culture of innovation and entrepreneurship. This was made possible by the fact that the CEO planned to stay in his position.

Strategically Choose which Fights to Fight

It is beneficial for new chief executive officers to introduce a small number of well-structured initiatives in a short amount of time. These initiatives can assist them in gaining momentum and signalling to audiences both inside and outside the organization the path they intend to pursue. By taking this strategy, you will not only be able to illustrate how and where you will concentrate your efforts but also establish a track record that will convince stakeholders to support your position. It provides you with the opportunity to achieve a few early victories while simultaneously laying the groundwork for the more significant strategic moves that you will later undertake.

How do you choose which aspect of your life to concentrate on first? From the very beginning, you will be inundated with demands from a variety of organizations, each of which will be conveyed with the utmost degree of urgency. As you work to establish confidence and garner support, you will naturally feel pushed to respond to all of these requests. Refuse to give in to that impulse, as it will put you on the path to failure in full force. Instead, make it a habit to decline the majority of requests, regardless of how interesting they may appear to be. Be methodical and begin with a modest step. It is necessary to determine which stakeholders should be given priority, select only a few of their most important needs and provide adequate attention to those demands.

One of the new CEOs that we worked with was completely overwhelmed by the sheer number of inquiries that she received upon her appointment to the position. Each problem was outlined to her as the most significant and pressing subject that she needed to address at the conclusion of the day. While she was taking stock of everything, she was overwhelmed. What was genuinely important and urgent? Not long after that, when we started working with her, we discovered that she had a difficult time treating all of the requests in the same manner. To assist her in breaking through that impasse, we sat down with her, mapped out all of the requests that she had received from the various stakeholders. We then worked with her to identify three primary and five secondary stakeholders whose issues she believed she could successfully respond to with a small set of early signature moves. Each of these moves was something that she was aware would earn the confidence of the stakeholders. She was able to act with purpose, communicate effectively and obtain input that would assist her in making subsequent actions because the process enabled her to be proactive rather than reactive. She was able to do this by focusing strategically on a small number of people rather than trying to reply to everyone. Be methodical and begin with a modest step. It is necessary to determine which stakeholders should be given priority, select only a few of their most important needs and provide adequate attention to those demands.

In a succession process that is well-managed, the new CEO will be given the opportunity to achieve early success by their predecessors. Within the context of one of the situations in which we were involved, the departing chief executive officer had recently bought a company and had purposefully left his successor with a clear mandate: integrating the two companies. During the first two years of her tenure as CEO, the new CEO enthusiastically embraced the task and deftly combined the two companies, both in terms of their operations and their cultures. The trust that she required for a more radical growth agenda was acquired by her as a result of that accomplishment, which she was then allowed to pursue in the years that followed.

Get Your Team in Sync

It is the most successful new CEOs who understand that in order to gain the confidence of others at an early stage, they must immediately concentrate on putting together a leadership team that is capable of high performance. However, it is all too often for new CEOs to put off getting this duty done, which does not garner as much attention as the introduction of exciting new projects does. Additionally, it may require them to make challenging decisions regarding senior individuals. This is the problem: if you do not have a team in place that is cohesive, in agreement on objectives and able to act successfully in support of your plans, it is nearly impossible to acquire the confidence of a large number of people.

Before attempting to get his top team on board with his goals, the new CEO that we worked with wanted to fill two critical roles first. This was before he attempted to get his top staff into agreement with his goals. It was his estimation that the searches would take a couple of months, at most three months. Nevertheless, as is sometimes the case, they took longer than anticipated, and while they were taking their time, another important executive departed the company, which resulted in yet another employee leaving their position. The fact that this CEO waited to begin moving forward lost him important time and gave the impression that he was both ineffectual and unable to make a decision.

There is no question that new CEOs who come from within the organization have a significant advantage because they have already established solid relationships within their respective companies. They must convince their former peers and colleagues, who have known them in other positions, that they have what it takes to lead the entire organization. This is a unique difficulty for the development of confidence, but it is also a one that they must overcome. For one CEO who had spent a significant portion of his lengthy career working for his company, this dilemma struck particularly close to heart he had. When he was promoted from Chief Financial Officer to Chief Executive Officer, he desired for the organization to have a more positive perception of him and to have a better understanding of him. In light of this, he freely disclosed more information about himself and his private life than he ever has before. He was candid about the ways in which he spent his weekends and the obstacles that he had to surmount, such as the serious illness that his child was experiencing. He was of the opinion that doing so was the most effective method for demonstrating his human side, rallying his staff behind him and allowing the organization to acquire faith in him.

When new CEOs are brought in from outside the organization, they are faced with a different dilemma. They have not yet been introduced to the organization, and stakeholders are keeping a close check on their every move as they attempt to comprehend their perspective within the organization. It was observed by one of the CEOs with whom we collaborated that everyone wants you to say something extravagant. Because of this, there is a strong tendency to give in to that and make statements that are bold. On the other hand, the more significant danger is in the possibility of being coerced into premature opinions, which could restrict your choices in the future and perhaps put you in a difficult position. It dawned on this chief executive officer that the uneasiness that came with being new to the position made him more likely to weigh in too fast and flaunt his intelligence. For the purpose of counteracting those tendencies, we collaborated with him to build a distinct executive agenda while simultaneously gaining an understanding of the core dimensions of the company, which would assist him in bringing all stakeholders together around the new road forward. It is important to involve stakeholders at the appropriate moment. In most cases, the board of directors is the first step in this process. In this context, establishing trust, familiarity and support is of utmost importance; nevertheless, new CEOs rarely realize how much time they will need to devote to mastering the nuances of boardroom dynamics and cultivating a strong relationship with each director. The new CEO devoted himself to this significant duty fairly immediately after he was appointed CEO. He was determined to gain an awareness not only of the domain competence of his individual directors, but also of their preferred engagement rhythms and styles of interaction. In order to get the directors acquainted with his senior team, he made arrangements for them to spend quality time together. This work paid off: at a time when many new CEOs become a bottleneck for information, he instead became an adept conductor of knowledge and was able to encourage his senior team to plan a course forward collaboratively. This was a significant accomplishment.

Gaining the confidence of each and every employee is likewise essential, and it need to be a routine that is followed every day. One strategy that is frequently successful is to hold regular "ask me anything" sessions with employee groups. The purpose of these sessions is to collect information about what people are thinking, how trends are developing and locations where the focus may need to be modified. This will not only assist you in gaining an understanding of the issues that your employees are concerned about but also provide them with the opportunity to feel heard, which is a natural way to build trust. It goes without saying that you must not overlook the obvious: in order to preserve that trust, you will need to make certain that your actions are consistent with the words that you utter, both in public and in private situations. It is also necessary for you to solicit investors. When it comes to a publicly traded corporation, the best time to begin is during the quarterly earnings calls. One newly appointed chief executive officer discovered the hard way that putting all of the emphasis on positive outcomes and bullish scenarios has a tendency to backfire, and when this occurs, it is detrimental to credibility. His strategy was rethought, and he started holding earnings calls. During these calls, he would provide a fair assessment of what was going well and what may go wrong. At the conclusion of the calls, he would spend time with analysts to get their opinions on the company. He discovered that investors' perceptions of him shifted, and they felt more confident in his ability to lead the company. This was due to the fact that he now appeared to be a careful steward of the company.

Everyone's attention is focused on the tasks that the new boss has to complete. On the other hand, the person who is leaving can make all the difference in the world.

Always Communicate Persistently and Clearly

It is essential to communicate effectively in order to instil confidence in your leadership across the many stakeholder groups. The question is, what is the most efficient approach to deal with it? Repetition. You will need to tell people what you are going to tell them, tell them and then tell them what you told them. This is true regardless of who you are speaking to or the context in which you are addressing them. Though exhausting, it is important to keep in mind that a significant portion of what you will be saying will either feel fresh to your audience or will begin to sink in only after a number of repeats.

Similarly, it is essential that you consistently communicate progress in all of your communications. Remind your stakeholders of from where you began, where you are currently and where you intend to go. In order to assist people in recognizing progress, you should divide your overall journey into smaller, more manageable portions that have objectives that are clearly measured. Your goals should be mapped against the calendar, and you should share your accomplishments in a reliable manner. Make any required adjustments to the course of action. Because of the changes that have taken place in your competitive environment, a plan that utilized a great deal of logic six months ago could no longer be able to do so. Your audiences should be informed on a frequent basis about the nature of such changes, and you should endeavour to ensure that they comprehend that you are making the appropriate modifications. This is yet another method that can be utilized to instill confidence in them over an extended period of time.

Get Better at Yourself

Because they have to service a large number of constituents, the majority of new CEOs do not prioritize their own education. That would be an error. Your ability to acquire the confidence of stakeholders and to create your own self-assurance more quickly will be facilitated by your continued investment in your own capabilities.

CEOs often do not have peers within the organization who are able to assist them in achieving this objective. Having a coach or an adviser who can regularly hold up the mirror, help them improve, present new insights and challenge their thinking is beneficial for the majority of presidents and chief executive officers, regardless of whether they are new or seasoned.

This was accomplished by putting a strong emphasis on the process of creating strategic goals for a new CEO. With an emphasis on discovering the areas in which her personal and organizational purposes overlapped, the approach started with her personal purpose and then expanded to include her organizational purpose. It was with our assistance and the participation of her inner circle of confidants, which included her heads of strategy and communications, that she was able to receive the constructive criticism and support that she needed in order to ensure that she could perform her job with self-assurance and a strong sense of purpose.

If you are a new chief executive officer, you will find that it is tempting to look for quick victories and to take dramatic moves that demonstrate a decisive behaviour. After starting a new job, you will feel a lot of exhilaration, but you will also feel a lot of pressure. On the other hand, the process of gaining the confidence and support of your stakeholders is neither a simple nor a quick one. Pacing yourself, strategically picking your battles, mobilizing your team, engaging stakeholders at the right time, communicating clearly and relentlessly, and investing in self-improvement are some of the steps that we have recommended in this chapter. By following these steps, you will be able to build confidence in your leadership over time and accelerate the transition from being the new CEO to simply being the CEO. To successfully navigate the complexity of leadership and maximize the value you produce over the long term, it will be essential for you to demonstrate patience, tenacity and continuous communication during your early years for leadership. It was many years ago when Bill Gates made the following statement, "We always overestimate the change that will occur in the next two years and underestimate the change that will occur in the next ten that will occur." Take care not to allow oneself to become lulled into passivity.

2

But Wait, Let's Listen to the Departing CEO

Every board hopes for a smooth transition of power when the CEO steps down, ideally one that is proactive and strategic and sets the company up for continued success. We all know the drill: get a head start, find and groom a pool of internal candidates, evaluate how well they mesh with the company's goals, pick the best one and then carefully integrate them.

Although the clinical focus on those processes is helpful, most succession studies have focused on the 'how.' What these studies often overlook are the feelings and behaviours of the exiting CEO, especially towards the end of the process.

The majority of CEOs fought for their position for a long time. They put in a lot of effort while in office to do things like improve operations, create the strategic direction and foster the firm's culture. Many CEOs see their position as more of an identity than a job. Directors should be mindful that leaving it can evoke strong emotions. There might be major repercussions for succession planning based on the emotions of departing CEOs. Based on our research, a smooth transition to a new CEO is more likely to occur when the outgoing CEO has a good rapport with the board, is involved in selecting their successor and has a positive outlook on the process. This is indicated by factors like the replacement's tenure and the rate of top-level employee turnover. Conflicts arise during transitions when departing CEOs feel ambivalent, regretful or left out of the successor selection process. The fragility of these changes is frequently disregarded by incumbents and boards.

Strong emotions are triggered even by perfectly planned CEO successions. After years of grooming her handpicked successor, Ursula Burns, to take over as CEO of Xerox, Anne Mulcahy handed the reins over to Burns in July 2009. The change was subsequently detailed by Mulcahy in the *Harvard Business Review*. According to her article published in October 2010, "Xerox's Former CEO on Why Succession Shouldn't Be a Horse Race," the current CEO is not given enough credit for the difficulty of the succession process. "It's not something you're born with, but it's meant to help you disappear without a trace."

We interviewed 30 former CEOs in depth to learn more about their experiences leaving the position. First, starting a succession; second, giving up control; third, controlling emotions; fourth, planning for the future; and fifth, emotionally and mentally disconnecting from the role and the organization are the five psychological crossroads that we identified through our research and synthesis of the data collected. Boards and new CEOs can better avoid issues if they are aware of the difficulties encountered by the outgoing leader at each of these junctures.

Initiating Succession

Our research shows that the majority of successions (83 per cent) were started by the CEO themselves. The top three reasons given for this were personal reasons, the organization's future demands, and age and tenure, which are considered temporal variables.

Although there was some variation in the exact years served or years left, the CEOs who departed for temporary reasons all used the phrase "feeling right" to describe their tenure or age range. "It was time after 16 years," remarked one former CEO of an executive advisory firm. Other CEOs who cited personal reasons stated that they had achieved their goals, lacked the energy or focus to continue in the role, or had ambitions outside of business. "Five years was kind of the right time frame," remarked one managing partner of a premier law firm.

Research on CEO succession has shown that some top executives struggle to step down from their positions because they feel their expertise is indispensable to the company or that they are impossible to replace. Contrary to what one might expect, our research shows that the reverse is really true: CEOs frequently start the succession process when they think about the future of the company. We were informed by leaders that there is a need for new perspectives or a different approach. The candidates' pipeline was another argument. "If I were to stay another five years, that would eliminate opportunities for others to continue progressing," stated the former head of a worldwide transportation company.

Relationships with the board were crucial to CEOs' readiness to initiate succession. The likelihood of CEOs initiating the procedure increased when it was robust. Directors still often pretended astonishment when told they were about to resign when they informed their boards of that. This shows that boards do talk about succession, but they aren't paying enough attention to when it might happen. "The board took a year to find a successor," remarked the former chief executive officer of a European investment management company.

It is concerning that most CEOs are starting the succession process, often catching the board by surprise. Directors would benefit from a better understanding of the factors that contribute to the desire to resign. The age and length of service of a CEO are public facts, so boards should be able to determine when it is appropriate to begin succession planning. Although directors and CEOs should communicate often, at least once a year, the board can use the temporal variables as a starting point for a discussion about the best time to do so. The fact that many executives are considering the talent pipeline as part of their retirement plans should encourage directors to be more forthright and honest with CEOs when discussing succession plans for the future. Boards might approach discussions with current CEOs about their expectations and timelines by focusing on the three primary reasons for departures: timing, organizational needs and personal needs. It is critical to cultivate strong ties with board members. CEOs who haven't done this often put off talking about their succession plans until they're ready to leave, making it tougher to have honest conversations. "I probably should have shifted some of the time I spent running the business to relationship building with the board," remarked the former CEO of a worldwide packaging company with a hint of regret. While it may come as a surprise, many CEOs have valid reasons for wanting to leave. These reasons can lead to positive discussions with the board that enhance the succession process as a whole, even if it means missing out on opportunities to spend time with my team.

Surrendering Authority

Canvassing for candidates, developing an ideal profile of their successor, conducting interviews, preparing applicants for the vetting process and finally, onboarding the chosen successor were the five types of succession activities that the CEOs we spoke with engaged in. Nevertheless, their participation frequently diminished as events progressed. Additionally, with the exception of the onboarding phase that follows the selection of a successor, nearly a quarter of CEOs (23 per cent) felt totally isolated from the process. Someone accustomed to being behind the wheel may find it unsettling. "Succession is our role, not yours," the board of directors of a utility business said to the outgoing chief executive officer when he brought up the subject during a board meeting. We don't require you to bring that up.

That perspective lacks long-term planning. "The CEO is really instrumental in a successful succession, even though in theory it's a board decision," stated the former CEO of a multinational financial services company, disregarding the opinions of corporate governance experts. Our findings indicate that chief executive officers have more faith in their successors' abilities to run the company when they are actively involved in the process of selecting them. We observed a favourable correlation between the prior CEO's involvement in the process and the length of a successor's term when looking at the 10 successors whose tenures ended after we finished data collection. However, transitions were more difficult when CEOs were either left out or had a small role. Five out of six transitions occurred when the CEO had engaged in either a single succession activity or none at all, and two of those transitions occurred after the CEO had departed without a successor in place. The extent to which a company's senior management stayed put following a CEO transfer was also influenced by the level of involvement of the departing CEO. The likelihood of senior executive defections decreased as the involvement of departing CEOs increased.

The loss of control that occurs during succession makes CEOs uneasy, and boards should understand this. This goes beyond a simple question of power; it raises the question of the significance of CEOs. Everyone, particularly those accustomed to positions of power, has a psychological need to feel important. The greater the CEO's involvement, the better the results will be for the organization, and boards should be aware of this. The succession process should be transparent in terms of who will be involved and how, and boards should maintain open lines of communication to define the CEO's role and the reasons for it. A leaving CEO's responsibilities include, but are not limited to, conducting candidate canvasses, developing a profile of a potential successor, helping applicants prepare for interviews and finally, onboarding the chosen individual. Another best practice for boards is to establish a transition plan with gates and succession measures.

As they move through the succession process, CEOs should be ready for a reduction in their role. Power battles prevent smooth transitions since people who don't expect this may try to regain control from the board. Executives should have a better understanding of the difficulties they are facing at this time if they are aware that their dwindling control is affecting their psychological need to matter. The best way for a departing CEO to feel at ease is to concentrate on the things they can do to make a difference, whether that's to themselves, their team or the company as a whole.

Controlling Feelings

CEOs, during transition, deal with the emotions of their successors and others around them.

From the viewpoint of the departing executives, half of the boards at the companies where we conducted our research were unresponsive when CEOs expressed their desire to stand down. Directors showed signs of surprise, worry about the timing or dissatisfaction with the news. Such replies caused the CEOs a great deal of distress and concern. In several instances, the boards of directors disagreed with the CEO's choice to leave on multiple occasions. In other instances, the boards deliberated the news for weeks before doing anything.

Managing the scepticism of key employees was another challenge for departing CEOs. When they stepped down, they frequently had to explain why. They needed to put people at ease regarding the implications of the new leadership on the team's and organization's future. Along with appointing their successors, departing CEOs also had to handle the disappointment of unsuccessful applicants. "The daggers got pointed back at me," remarked the ex-CEO of an institutional investment venture. "We had a deep relationship based on trust and a history of 20 years of working together, so I felt very connected to them. Somehow, they were furious."

The CEOs' own complex emotions were another factor. Feelings of isolation and dishonesty from having to keep the news a secret accompanied the difficult time between deciding to step down and making the announcement. According to a former health care CEO, "I was specifically told that I couldn't make an announcement, even though in my mind there was an end date for my job in this company...My genuine intentions had to be concealed at all costs."

CEOs went through a range of emotions when they announced their resignation, from joy to sadness. The fact that they could now come clean about their choice was, on the one hand, a relief. The idea of a suitable successor taking over was exciting to some. "It was a thrill, like passing the baton to the proper person," remarked the former real estate services firm CEO. However, CEOs often felt helpless and saddened by their departure from the position, and they were also irritated by their limited participation in and understanding of the succession planning process. Concerned for the organization's and their successor's future, they fretted. Some people felt accountable if things went wrong, which caused them to feel guilty in advance.

Most notably, CEOs felt let down and surprised by how rapidly their importance was diminished as support moved to the next in line. A number of outgoing CEOs also reported feeling disrespected when their successors or replacements received more publicity than they did for their own contributions to the company. During a single call, the board not only announced the departure of the departing CEO but also presented and highlighted the credentials of the new CEO.

Exiting executives appeared to be better able to manage their negative feelings when the CEO-board connection was robust, as was the case at the other crossroads. But CEOs still had a hard time even when they took the lead in starting and participating in the succession process.

Boards' Guidance

Executives may go through a wide range of emotions, and boards should be prepared for it. Certain times (like the preannouncement phase) are known to be more difficult than others, and they should be aware of this. The board of directors has a responsibility to see how the chief executive officer is doing and to mitigate any distress that may result from the transition (for example, by reducing the time the departing CEO has to conceal the news of their leave). The board of directors should keep their emotions in check in light of the CEO's resignation.

CEOs should not repress their emotions but rather lean into them and seek to comprehend their significance; this will help them manage their own emotional journey. A professional coach, a fellow CEO, the chief human resources officer or even a spouse are all trustworthy third parties with whom you might benefit from discussing these matters. "It's important to be honest about what your emotional vulnerabilities are going to be and what your safety net will be," warned the former CEO of a transportation solutions firm. "And you need to be candidly raw, be able to say, 'I need help today.'" The executives we spoke with also suggested that departing CEOs keep stakeholders (such as their own teams, customers and partners) informed of the succession plan in order to reduce confusion and provide more clarity. There will always be emotions in the boardroom, even though some people think they don't belong there. The key to a smooth succession is being prepared for them, being aware of when and where to seek help and anticipating their needs.

Getting Ready for What Comes Next

Many chief executive officers fail to bring the same level of strategic thinking to their personal lives that they bring to the company. We found that 53 per cent of the CEOs we surveyed had no strategy for their post-employment life. Even though departing CEOs knew it was important to think about what to do next, they often found that pressing day-to-day tasks consumed all of their mental energy. Our findings that CEOs who failed to prepare for the shift reported higher levels of unpleasant feelings are perhaps not unexpected.

According to Yale University's Jeffrey Sonnenfeld, who conducted the last empirical study on CEO turnover in the 1980s, "in contemplating their own retirement, [CEOs] see only losses." Sonnenfeld noted that few CEOs mentioned their hobbies or leisure activities. Bill George, a former chief executive and current professor at Harvard Business School, wrote an article for the *Harvard Business Review* in 2019 titled "The CEO's Guide to Retirement." George said that current CEOs have more options than ever before for active and meaningful retirements, such as serving on boards for businesses or nonprofits, publishing books, working for private equity firms, starting foundations, working for government or mentoring upcoming leaders. This time of generativity is tremendously gratifying, according to many previous CEOs, George stated. As a matter of fact, every single one of the ex-CEOs that participated in our study was either working full-time, part-time or very involved in some other capacity or endeavour when we interviewed them.

Leadership

Leaving the position of CEO doesn't always imply leaving the company altogether. Again, a good relationship with the board increased the likelihood that the departing CEO would stick on as a board member or coach for the new CEO, but nearly half of all CEOs stayed on in some way following the handover. Retaining a predecessor in some capacity can be challenging for a new chief executive officer, but studies have shown that when a CEO steps down, their moods improve and they lose less key employees.

How the departing CEO should continue to be involved after formally stepping down is one of the most important issues that a board must make. It is more realistic for the departing CEO to remain on as a board or advisor when the replacement intends to maintain the same strategy while making small adjustments. The departing CEO may be seen by the incoming CEO as a roadblock by those with more ambitious plans for change. The successor and the board must reach a unanimous conclusion on this matter.

An effective strategy for directors to assist a retiring CEO is to draw on their own experiences with leaving a high-level position, particularly if they are themselves past CEOs. They can be a sounding board, provide networking assistance or advise to incoming CEOs as they face this difficult transition. The change can be lessened by human interaction on a shared journey and at significant rest breaks along the way out.

Having a diverse set of interests is important for CEOs in our study, both while they are in office and after they stand down. Some were more at ease with structure and planning as they prepared for life after CEO, while others preferred to start fresh. The majority of leaders have stressed that the next act must centre on core purpose. Lastly, numerous CEOs emphasized the need to refrain from hastily filling their schedules without thoroughly considering their future aspirations.

Stepping Away from the Position and the Company

Outgoing chief executive officers often struggle to separate themselves from their position and officially surrender the title of chief executive officer. Based on our data, we found that 43 per cent of CEOs perceived their role as their identity and 47 per cent as their work. The remaining 51 per cent felt a mix of the two. Given the way others reacted to them, it was frequently difficult to refrain from associating one's identity with the CEO role, even though some were cognizant of the risks. People kept treating former chief executives as though they were still in charge, even after they stepped down. "People come up to me and talk to me as if I'm still the CEO," mentioned the former head of a multinational financial organization. "Sometimes other CEOs will phone me and say there's a problem. In response, I clarify that I did in fact retire eight years ago."

One of the most important things a board can do is choose a new CEO. However, it is common for directors, current leaders and incoming leaders to fail to fully grasp the complexity of the leadership transition.

In order to mark the end of the tenure of departing chief executive officers and honour their achievements, boards should think about organizing a ceremony or finding other ways to do it. These kinds of things can make people feel good, fulfil their ego demands and help them move on. According to anthropologists, rituals have always been a way for humans to deal with the unknown that comes with major life changes. No big budget is required if this is to be held as an event; what matters is that it has significance. "I got two inches' worth of letters from employees saying what they were thankful for, and they did a surprise send-off," the former CEO of a technology company described to us. That had a profoundly beneficial effect on me. Unexpected, genuine, and satisfying, it's hard to put a price on happiness.

Our conversations with CEOs reinforced the need of maintaining a healthy separation between one's professional and personal lives. "Start thinking about that early because the relationship to that piece of identity is going to shift," advised the former CEO of an insolvency services firm. That begs the question, how are you going to break free of that identity? How are you going to forge a new trajectory for yourself?

Our research shows that CEOs who adopt a servant leadership style are more likely to see themselves as being at the very bottom of the corporate ladder and to define themselves in relation to their personal lives outside of work. Although their transitions were less rocky, some of those leaders were nevertheless taken aback by how suddenly they were cut off. Some people are disappointed by how quickly they are forgotten, according to a former executive of a professional sports firm. The individuals we talked to advised CEOs to seek out professional coaches, peer groups, and others who had been through the same thing as a way to deal with this new reality.

The importance of the exiting CEO's emotions and behaviours to successions is often underappreciated, both in theory and in practice. This trend hurts boards, successors who are trying to take over and departing CEOs (who often feel alone during this transition). The organization would benefit from a seamless transfer from the outgoing CEO, and boards can take some measures to improve the chances of this happening.

All succession crossroads are far easier to manage when there are deep and genuine relationships between the exiting CEO and individual board members. This is the most effective counsel for everyone involved. Furthermore, such connections should be established well in advance of the changeover. According to a former chief executive officer of a home appliance firm, "You can have more awkward conversations because there is trust when CEOs and directors have a long history of personal relationships." Throughout a CEO's career, cultivating these connections should be a constant top concern.

3

With Greater Power, Comes Greater Responsibility

There are five pitfalls that you should steer clear of as you gain power as a leader.

The older you become, the more hilarious your jokes will get, according to an old proverb. Power, on the other hand, has the ability to alter you. Your views, judgement and behaviour are all impacted as a result. It is not often understood that power does not only affect you, but it also influences individuals who are in your immediate vicinity. When someone holds power, they make themselves a target for the expectations and projections of other people. When someone assumes a position of authority, they are no longer regarded as an individual but rather as a representation of command and control. Your ideas might be overvalued by people, while theirs might be undervalued. As a result, the feedback they provide to you might be less honest and less accurate. There is a possibility that they will be less reluctant to speak up, trust their judgements and take chances, and they may also choose to ignore your inappropriate behaviour. Additionally, they may have exaggerated expectations regarding what you are capable of accomplishing, or they may view you with scepticism, hoping to determine whether or not you are deserving of the status that you already have.

What is the end result? In ways that you might not even be aware of, you are shaped by the way other people react to your power. If you are not conscious of this dynamic, you run the risk of falling into the traps that your power generates, which will undermine your capacity to do what is right for the organization and accomplish what you want to accomplish. It has been demonstrated through research that when leaders misuse their authority, the motivation of their followers decreases and their intents to contribute to their organizations to the fullest extent possible also decrease.

The purpose of this chapter is to provide an overview of some primary power. It is true that these pitfalls can put leaders at any level in danger; but, the longer you have been in a position of authority, the more intense and potentially dangerous they can become than they were before. While you may not be able to control how other people react to you, you do have the ability to regulate your own behaviour and implement techniques that will help you reduce the negative effects of the shifting power dynamic. Your mission is to make the most of your power so that it serves you rather than working against you.

Snare of the Saviour

When you are recognized as the expert, you run the risk of falling into the trap of providing advice frequently, having all the answers and being overly helpful. Being a blowhard who always weighs in, even on things that are outside of your area of expertise, is one manifestation of this. Another manifestation is being the saviour for every challenge, to the point where your team is rendered incapable. Attempting to solve everyone's issues, micromanaging projects or goods and providing suggestions that are not required or that are outside of your scope are all examples of behaviours that are indicative of falling into the saviour trap.

What kind of an issue is this? You have an inflated sense of self-confidence when you are engrossed in the process of rescuing other people. The fact that you feel the need to be helpful or to exert control makes you a single point of collapse. In addition, you are preventing others from providing valuable input, thus restricting their capacity to contribute or develop, making it possible for others to experience a diminished sense of self-reliance or accountability.

For the purpose of avoiding falling into the saviour trap of power and ensuring that your skill does not become out of control, the following methods will be of assistance. First, ask questions before you respond. Develop the practice of asking one question before providing an answer to a question. Second, always tell the truth to yourself. What percentage of the ideas and proposals that you communicate to your colleagues during a meeting actually end up being put into action? In situations where people are competent but apprehensive about a goal or assignment, it is important to actively listen to their concerns and promote issue solutions. You might ask your peers to score the value of your suggestions in an anonymous and confidential manner. Not only do these supporting behaviours have a beneficial impact on the motivation and growth of employees, but they also prevent you from having to play the position of evangelist.

The Trap of Being Complacent

When you are in a position of authority, you are frequently the single most knowledgeable person in the room. Nevertheless, in contrast to the saviour trap, the complacency trap is characterized by a diminishing level of curiosity. As a result of your belief that you are completely knowledgeable, you ask less questions. It is assumed that you have a good understanding of the issue, yet you do not inquire further. From your perspective, silence is synonymous with agreement, and you presume that agreement is more than just compliance.

In the event that you allow yourself to become complacent, you will not be able to discover the truth because you have not actively sought out a more in-depth conversation. The questions "Am I missing something?" and "What might I have overlooked?" have not been the ones you have asked. In the event that someone seeks assistance from you, you provide them with the solution rather than asking them questions such as "What have you tried?" or "What do you think the problem is?"

What kind of an issue is this? You run the danger of missing out on the knowledge and data that you require in order to make sound judgements when you remain complacent. In addition, you are not assisting your team in developing critical thinking skills and the ability to solve problems independently.

By engaging in the following techniques, you will be able to successfully traverse the complacent trap of power and resist your laxity, thereby ensuring that you do not overlook important bits of information.

Establish a method of inquiry that reveals the assumptions, values and beliefs that are inherent in the conversation. Inquire, "What assumptions are we drawing from here? Which questions haven't been asked yet? What are some things that an external stakeholder, rival or client might discover that we have not yet taken into consideration?"

During your conversations, you should employ the 'five whys' strategy in order to combat complacency. The inquiry 'why' should be asked whenever someone brings up a problem or asks a question until you have arrived at the underlying cause of the issue or a deeper layer of the problem.

In order to prevent complacency from ever being the norm and to make continual learning a value, you should make it a point to actively communicate what you now know.

Always be present. This can be a sign of distraction, which is the outcome of multitasking and being inattentive. Complacency might be this symptom. When you are having a conversation with someone, put down your phone. You should put away your electronic devices and ask questions if you are at a meeting. By doing so, you will improve your presence, and consequently, your curiosity, and, as a result, demonstrate to other people that what they have to say and what they have to offer is significant.

The Catch-22 of Avoidance

Shortcuts are possible when one is in a position of authority. Despite the fact that it provides you with increased autonomy, options and possibilities, it also enables you to avoid unpleasant jobs by delegating them to other people or, if at all possible, avoiding them entirely. It is possible to avoid having a difficult conversation or providing feedback that is difficult. There is a quarrel that is brewing on your squad, but you may ignore it. Due to the fact that calling out unpleasant behaviour is uncomfortable; you can choose to ignore it.

What kind of an issue is this? You could feel less burdened in the short term if you avoid the unpleasant aspects of your position, but in the long run, it will only dull you. When you avoid challenging tasks, your capacity to complete them on your own will gradually diminish. Atrophy begins to occur in the emotional muscles that are responsible for managing discomfort, resolving conflicts and listening with an open mind to those who have opposing points of view.

When a leader chooses the duties they are responsible for, they are also sending the message that being accountable to their duty is not expected of them. They have a reputation for being unreliable, and it is widespread knowledge that a lack of dependability leads to a reduction in trust in leaders and, ultimately, in the organization that permits it.

In order to successfully navigate the power avoidance trap and turn towards rather than away from challenges, the following practices will be of great assistance:

Consider the responsibilities that come with your position. What are the requirements for the role? Do I have to do this? Is it necessary for me to finish this task?

- Give some thought to the consequences of your inaction, including the consequences for yourself, for others, for your team and for the firm. What are the repercussions that will occur if you do not take action to address the issue? What kind of examples are you creating for your staff that will end up costing you money in the long run? Because you are avoiding it, are you reducing the amount of work you have to do or increasing it?
- Make the mental shift from one in which stress is detrimental to your well-being to one in which stress is beneficial. One's perspective on the difficulty of the task has an effect on the level of stress that it causes. By cultivating the perspective that stress is helpful and that confronting challenging situations will make you a stronger leader, you will be less likely to avoid duties that are unpleasant to you.

We avoid undertaking things that we believe we are not capable of performing. Make a list of the duties that are needed of you in your work but that you would rather avoid or that you have a tendency to put off until later. Acquire the services of a coach or mentor who will go over the list and determine the abilities that are need to tackle each element. You should make sure that this person serves as your mentor and holds you accountable for learning those abilities.

A Trap Set by Friends

When leaders have difficulty taking ownership of the power that comes with their position, they run the risk of falling into the friend trap with their direct reports. This may be an uncomfortable environment to be in. Acting as if you are a peer when you are not is an example of the friend trap. In an effort to be liked and to reduce the magnitude of their authority footprint, these leaders place an excessive amount of reliance on their personal strength and forego the power that comes with their position. When someone receives a promotion and is then placed in the position of managing their former colleague, we observe this phenomenon. It is possible that the new leader will have difficulty holding people accountable or making choices. In addition, they might divulge personal information or show favouritism, both of which are activities that are known to generate uncertainty and turmoil.

What kind of an issue is this? It is just as much an act of omission (failing to do the right thing) as it is an act of commission (doing something bad) when authority is abused. When leaders fail to demonstrate the power that comes with their position, those around them are unable to comprehend what is required of them, which hinders their capacity to concentrate and carry out their duties. In addition, failing to fulfil the responsibilities that come with your authority creates a void that is frequently filled by the most dominant member of your team, who is not necessarily the most capable member, which results in tension and conflict.

In order to avoid falling into the power trap of friends and to fulfil your positional authority, the following practices will be of assistance:

- Make a note of the reasons why you were promoted; it is quite likely that you possess the talents necessary to live up to the responsibilities of your post. Putting together a list of the reasons why you are the ideal candidate for the position and posting it in a location where you can easily access it is a good idea.
- Strive to achieve harmony with authority. As a result of all the ways in which they have witnessed authority being misused, we are aware that a great number of individuals are at ease when it comes to power. Take into consideration those in your life or in the public realm who make excellent use of the influence they possess. How do they accomplish what they do that makes them so successful? What are some attitudes or behaviours that you could try to incorporate into your life?
- Conduct an inventory of all of your strengths and decide how you can best utilize them for the role you are applying for. When you take your personal abilities for granted, it is simple to use them in a random manner rather than exercising them with intention. Any strength, even congeniality, has the potential to become a liability if it is exaggerated.

The new relationships and obligations that you have with your team should be explicitly chartered. On certain projects, you might want to think about utilizing a decision-making framework. You will be able to eliminate any uncertainty and ambiguity regarding the manner in which you will utilize the power that comes with your new position.

A Catch-22 for Stress

As a result of the immense amount of pressure that is placed on leaders to generate results, leadership is inherently stressful. Uncertainty and instability are always present because of the rapid pace of technological progress and the changeable conditions of the market. In addition, many leaders are pressed for time between employees and senior leadership, working to meet deadlines and deliverables while also coping with budget cuts and personnel churn.

Stress that is not properly managed creates negative consequences not just for the leader who is experiencing it but also for those who are in their immediate vicinity. The act of sending emails in the middle of the night, responding angrily to requests or micromanaging out of fear are all examples of behaviours that contribute to "second-hand stress," which is the act of passing on your emotional condition to other people. This is emphasized by the fact that you have authority over this situation. When you are the boss, you might think that you are simply being a bit grouchy, but to the other person, you are TEXTING in all capital letters. It is okay for everyone to have a terrible day when they are in charge.

What kind of an issue is this? It is possible for your direct reports to minimize negative news or neglect to tell you when things aren't going well until it is too late. This is done in order to avoid being in the firing line of your workplace stress. People are unable to think effectively and creatively when they are in an environment that is overwhelming. An alarmingly high number of studies have demonstrated that exposure to second-hand stress can even raise the risk of coronary artery disease in workers.

It is possible to avoid falling into this power trap and to manage your stress in such a way that you do not cause it for other people by engaging in the following practice:

- Come up with a list of activities that you can do to manage stress, such as practicing mindfulness, breathing or relaxation techniques, cognitive-behavioural therapy or other mind-body approaches.

You can lessen and better manage your stress by making changes to your everyday habits. Make sure to take breaks in between meetings, engage in physical activity, maintain a healthy diet and schedule short breaks after periods of intense work. Through effective management of your energy, you can not only enhance your mental well-being but also become more productive and contribute to the overall productivity of your team. There is a certain amount of stress that cannot be avoided; thus, you should postpone writing a demanding email or replying to a challenging request until you have had sufficient time to reflect, discuss the situation with someone else or go for a walk. It is also possible to restrict your email and other forms of communication to workday hours (for instance, from nine in the morning until five in the afternoon). This not only shows that you respect the boundaries of others but also provides you with additional time to ponder and obtain some space from your feelings.

One of the problems associated with positional power is that these traps are, to a certain extent, unavoidable. It is expected of you to provide responses and to contribute your level of experience. Because of the position you hold, you are able to bypass some of the "grunt work" so that you may focus on serving as a leader. To a certain extent, you should be convivial, but you should avoid being authoritative, in order to motivate and assist your team.

Despite this, it is a precarious situation. In addition, if you are not vigilant, any one of these pitfalls has the potential to erode the credibility and effectiveness of your leadership. In the event that you receive feedback indicating that you are caught in one of these power dynamics, or if you become aware that you are too dependent on a comfort that your position gives you, we encourage you to try with a tool that corresponds to your situation. When you improve the way in which you wield the authority that comes with your position, you give others around you more agency, you create conditions that are conducive to growth and you improve the outcomes for the organization.

4

Employee is Distressed! What Should a CEO Do?

You pass the cubicle of an employee. While he rests his forehead on his hands, he has his elbows resting on his desk. He gives off an anxious vibe. Do you dare to speak up? If so, how would you go about it?

Carefully dealing with employees' unpleasant emotions is a critical and challenging leadership skill. Anger, sadness and depression are common workplace emotions, and knowing how to respond appropriately (or not) may have a profound impact on your employees' mental health, your relationship with them and the team's productivity. Leaders can respond to employees' emotions in ways that support their health and the culture and effectiveness of their organizations, according to our research on workplace emotions and our work with numerous global organizations, such as PepsiCo, Oracle, Exxon Mobil and General Motors.

We found that the most effective leaders pay great attention to their employees' needs in the workplace, such as belonging, purpose, and feeling valued and connected, and respond to their emotions in ways that help them achieve those needs. On top of that, they are adept at knowing when to offer counsel, when to just listen, and when to allow workers space to work through their emotions on their own.

Here, leaders' decisions matter. Leaders' words and actions when they observe their staff are distressed, irritated or overwhelmed can have far-reaching repercussions, according to a 2024 analysis of 220 studies on the topic. Separately, in 2018 we investigated how leaders' responses to staff members' emotions affected team output. A difficult decision-making assignment was put to 190 teams. Half of the teams were given specific instructions and a variety of suggestions for how to make sure their leaders acknowledged their employees' feelings during team discussions. Someone could comment, "Hey, I noticed you seem to be down." or ask, "How are you feeling about that decision?" if they noticed someone was sad. It was told to the other teams' captains not to show any emotion. What was the outcome? There was a marked improvement in performance for teams whose leaders took the time to acknowledge the feelings of their members.

In this chapter, we provide leaders with a framework for helping their staff cope emotionally. But first, I'd want to clear up three frequent misunderstandings.

Myth No. 1: It Is Unprofessional to Talk About Feelings and Things at Work

It is the belief of many managers that employees' ability to focus on their task is negatively impacted when they are able to express their feelings on the job. The long-held belief that employees should not show their feelings on the job may be the root cause of this. Totaljobs, an online recruiting site, polled 2,250 UK workers in October 2019 and found that 51 per cent of managers believe employees should keep their emotions in check while on the clock. Expressing emotions on the job has long been stigmatized as "unprofessional," especially in Western nations.

There may be some small benefits to ignoring other people's feelings every once in a while, but the big rewards much outweigh them. As an example, research conducted by Alisa Yu, Justin Berg, and Julian Zlatev in 2021 showed that showing empathy towards coworkers' feelings (by saying something like, "I can understand why you might be worried about the deadline" or "You seem to be a bit down" can foster trust. Going out of your way to check in shows that you're ready to invest in the individual and the connection. Management teams that encouraged members to express and respond to their emotions performed better than teams that expected members to keep their emotions in check, according to a field study and two lab trials published in 2022 by Michael Parke and colleagues.

Basically, leaders who aren't afraid to tap into their employees' emotions are less likely to lead by example and more likely to see their teams succeed professionally.

Myth No. 2: It is too Risky to Get Involved in People's Private Lives

For fear of appearing to meddle in their employees' private lives, many leaders avoid dealing with their team members' emotions. Worried about appearing or saying the wrong thing, they could also be unsure of how to react appropriately.

But emotions are the links that bind us to one another. Making an effort to understand and empathize with your employees' feelings shows them that you value their well-being and that you are concerned about their situation. A simple "I'm here for you" message, a compliment, a joke or a thoughtful gesture like a cookie or flower left on a desk can go a long way towards helping an employee who is struggling.

Start with smaller gestures, like recognizing the tension in the room during a difficult meeting, if you're worried about crossing boundaries by asking your colleagues how they're feeling. As an example, at one meeting we were a part of, the leader made a point of looking up at an employee who had been wounded by a coworker's remark and then winked and smiled to show that she knew how the employee felt. By doing so, he was able to control his emotions and return to the conversation with renewed vigour.

Myth No. 3: When People Express Their Feelings to You, They Really Want You to Fix Their Problems.

A lot of people believe that leaders should also deal with issues that are making employees unhappy as they are supposed to repair things at work. So, instead of listening to their staff and trying to figure out what they need, they just jump in and give advise. About 80 per cent of the time, leaders try to alter people's feelings instead of accepting them, according to our published research.

There are times when employees just want to tell their leaders what's going on and be understood, even though they may really want their leaders' assistance with a problem at times. When employees open up about how they're feeling, managers should be mindful of their solution-oriented bias and pay close attention to their needs.

A Structure for Efficient Reactions

First, there are two connected questions to ask when dealing with an employee's emotions: (1) Is the employee appearing to be coping? (2) Does your worker have an urgent task at hand? Among four possible strategies, the best one will be determined by the responses.

Situation A: Your Employee Appears to be Handling Things Well and Isn't Concentrating on a Deadline-Driven Task

Envision this: when you say goodbye to your employee Alex in the parking lot, he brings up the fact that he's been feeling very depressed about everything at work. He seems open to talking about his feelings, but he isn't asking for or seeking your assistance. Here, it's best to just listen without offering advise; just let him know that you're there and that his feelings are OK.

Here, you might take a number of different techniques. Saying something like, "It really makes sense why you would feel that way," will help validate his emotions and reassure him that they're normal. On the other hand, you may ask him, "From your perspective, what happened to make you feel this way? It has been tough." This would demonstrate that you're interested in understanding what's making him so downhearted.

This is where remembering that individuals often come to us to air their grievances without really wanting our advize becomes crucial. Perhaps all they really need is for a coworker to make them feel valued and understood. Unfortunately, we tend to step in and attempt to solve their problems without being specifically asked to do so.

Situation B: Your Employee Appears to be Emotionally Handling a Time-Sensitive Job Goal

Imagine Diego, who is still reeling over the loss of his dog but must now face an emotionally charged audience in order to make a critical presentation. Recognizing his unhappiness at this moment could undermine his efforts by unleashing a torrent of emotions he has briefly attempted to contain, even though he might value your concern in another context.

The moment to intervene is not when people seem to be able to control their emotions while attending to critical tasks.

"You seem nervous" or "Don't worry—this is not a big deal" or inquiring, "Are you feeling all right?" are not appropriate responses.

Do not rush into checking in after the critical activity has been finished; instead, wait for a chance to show your care and offer assistance if needed.

Situation C: Your Employee is Suffering Emotionally While Working on a Critical, Time-Sensitive Assignment

You are required to step in when an employee requests or obviously requires assistance. Our interviewee, an attending surgeon, told us that she had to help the resident doctors on her team manage their emotions on the spot when they're visibly terrified during challenging procedures. To help them relax, she will say something encouraging, such as, "I'm confident in your abilities; trust your training" or gently remind them to concentrate. She will then either take on the difficult work alone or assign it to another member of the surgical team if that isn't sufficient.

There are a variety of strategies that can be implemented when individuals are under intense strain and want prompt assistance in managing their emotions in order to concentrate on a crucial activity. One is to offer some encouragement, whether in the form of a joke, a compliment or reassurance, to break the negative cycle that could lead to them, their team and the mission's derailment. According to a Navy SEAL commander we spoke with, if he sees a teammate emotionally struggling, he will wait for a quiet moment and approach them, giving them words of encouragement like "You can do this" or a joke. The coach will tell the teammate to hang in there and then keep an eye on them to see if they need any more help focusing.

What is your default response? For instance, you might be prone to going into solution mode far too soon, as many people do.

When someone aren't handling things properly, how can you tell? Their expressions, voice tone, posture, breathing patterns or lack of concentration will probably have to suffice to indicate that they need assistance, even though they may ask for it directly.

Once a work is finished, leaders should also make sure to check in with their personnel. As you guide others in emotional regulation and goal attainment, you run the risk of unintentionally implying that their feelings were unwarranted or that your concern for them is superficial. So, after taking action, it's important to clarify your reasoning and express your appreciation for their feelings. "I wanted to help you focus since that was a critical point in the surgery, but I want to check in now to see how you're doing—that was a tough procedure." This approach can make someone feel seen and heard, which can contribute to a better team culture, according to the attending surgeon.

Situation D: The Person Isn't Completing a Task That Requires Immediate Attention, But they Aren't Coping Either

Just pretend you and Melissa are having a meeting. Despite the lack of an immediate deadline, she expresses her feelings of being overwhelmed, confused about how to proceed and anxious about maybe having to abandon initiatives that she is enthusiastic about. You should take a moment to address her emotions rather than responding with a problem-solving statement like, "Well, here's how I manage such situations..." or worse, changing the subject or ignoring what she has said. She isn't in the middle of an urgent task, so there's time to do it.

The most effective way for a leader to help an employee is to be able to do both things at the same time, which is accepting the emotion and then doing something to change the mood. One example is the work of Lisanne Pauw and colleagues, who conducted two studies in which participants were asked to pretend they were having a conversation with a friend while feeling a strong unpleasant emotion. The next step was to have them rate how helpful it was when the buddy did one of three things: either accepted the emotion without offering any assistance, offered assistance after accepting the emotion or both. Which answer got the best score? First, you must acknowledge the emotion; and second, you must assist in resolving the issue that is triggering it.

After a devastating loss, you can employ this strategy to keep your team's emotions in check, much like the iconic coach Ted Lasso did in the namesake Apple TV+ series. "This is a sad moment right here," he said to the squad, recognizing their emotions. For everyone here. "No amount of words I can utter right now will ever be able to erase that," he said, before telling his team to take a deep breath, collect themselves and concentrate on the next game.

Improving Your Abilities

Our research has shown that there are three paths that leaders may take to become better at easing the emotional strain on their staff.

Figure Out What You Usually Do

What is your default response? If so, know that you are not isolated. Having a one-size-fits-all attitude towards everyone is a prevalent pattern of behaviour. For instance, you might be prone to going into solution mode far too soon, as many people do.

Be mindful of your actions in diverse situations to fight against that propensity. Is your reaction appropriate for every circumstance?

Keep an eye on how people are reacting, as well as your own. Were the workers you were concerned about showing appreciation? Were you given any suggestions on how to improve your response to them or others in the future? From their response, can you infer what they require? Ask questions.

Observe how other people react to your emotions and take that knowledge with you. When you're down and out and all you want is someone to acknowledge your feelings, how does it feel when they advise you to pull yourself together? That feeling when someone notices your feelings and checks in with you to see how you're doing?

Learn New Things

Having a repertoire of responses to pick from is necessary for handling employees' emotions in a context-appropriate manner. Yours can be enriched by taking note of how other people react to other's emotions. Perhaps one coworker has excellent advice, and another knows just what to say to get you to think about things from a new angle.

You should attempt experimenting with new and improved methods as soon as you see them. Every interaction, no matter how ordinary, is a chance to practise positive social skills; for example, you may offer a smile to a sad-looking customer or apologize for frustrating them when you hold up the queue. You can practise handling an angry teammate in a low-stakes situation by conducting these types of mini-experiments.

Leaders should have the emotional intelligence to respond to their staff in a way that boosts their morale. That calls for students to develop their abilities, become more self-aware and learn to deal with the emotions of others in a variety of settings. An improved and healthier organization is the outcome of their mastery of those three elements.

5

Playing Favourites? No, Strictly No

During our most recent engagement with a Scandinavian robotics business, we came across a concerning piece of information: the CEO of the company primarily addressed and conferred with only three of his nine executives during meetings of the leadership team, while the remaining employees passively observed. When we confronted him about this dynamic at a later time, he was taken aback. He was astonished to learn that he had discernible "favourites," and he was also ignorant of the influence that his favouritism might have on the other executives. During the upward feedback exercises, the problem had never been brought up before.

This is a situation that occurs far too frequently. As much as the majority of managers believe that they treat every person of their team with the same amount of attention, respect and concern, empirical research conducted over the course of forty years reveals that this is not the case. On the other hand, studies have shown that almost all managers have in-groups with whom they have warmer, more personal interactions and out-groups with whom they function more transactionally. This is the perception that is held by the majority of managers. There is also evidence to suggest that when individuals find themselves on the wrong side of these divisions, it has a negative impact on their engagement, job happiness, dedication and ultimately, their ability to collaborate, innovate and do quality work.

Subordinates pay great attention to how they are treated in comparison to colleagues who are of equivalent talent, work ethic and status. This is true regardless of the function, organization, industry or area in which they are employed. Different leaders' tones, sincerities, body language, styles, emotional support, flexibility, criticism and praise are easily discernible to them. They are fast to recognize these differences. And when they observe or have the impression that a manager is less likely to solicit their opinions, build on their suggestions, encourage their initiatives, notice their efforts or take into consideration their needs and preferences—as if they work for the person rather than with them—they frequently become disillusioned, distressed and even hostile. "My boss referred to me as a 'valuable resource,' and he meant it as a compliment," said one executive who shared their thoughts with us. Given the glowing adjectives he had used to characterize other members of the team, I can tell you that it did not make me feel particularly human or respected. And I can say this with certainty. There have been some individuals who have been brought to tears by the favouritism of managers; there have been others who have screamed about it outside of the team, which has damaged everyone's standing; and there have been many individuals who have simply quit in pursuit of an in-group elsewhere, even if it meant taking a wage cut.

The majority of the time, managers will say that any divergence is unintentional and that their reports put an excessive amount of emphasis on relatively minor differences. Both assertions might be correct. The perspective from below, on the other hand, is the one that matters. Real repercussions can result from a perception of unfairness. Therefore, it is of the utmost importance that managers first acknowledge these problems and then make a concerted effort to either prevent or resolve disagreements. If they do not, they run the risk of losing key contributors, making the obstacles that are presented by underachievers much more difficult to overcome, destroying the performance and morale of the team, and damaging their own reputations.

Comprehending the Problem at Hand

A study that was conducted in 2006 by Joe Labianca and Daniel Brass, both of whom were professors at the University of Kentucky Gatton School of Business, discovered that eight per cent of the connections that occurred in the workplace were completely negative. On the other hand, new findings regarding employee engagement and the impact of supervisors on voluntary departure indicate that the issue extends much beyond that in terms of the relationship between supervisors and subordinates.

A survey conducted by Gallup in 2023 with more than 120,000 employees revealed that 59 per cent of respondents reported feeling disengaged, which is a group that the pollsters and others have referred to as "quiet quitters." Additionally, 18 per cent of respondents stated that they were actively disengaged, which is a term that refers to individuals who were vocal about their unhappiness and likely to demoralze their colleagues. It is important to note that although supervisors are not the sole element that drives employee engagement, they are a significant one. In a survey conducted by McKinsey in 2021, for instance, it was shown that 52 per cent of those who left their positions did so in part because they did not feel valued by their superiors.

To this day, the majority of researchers who have studied boss-subordinate relationships, also known as leader-member interchange, have concentrated mostly on the advantages that come with high-quality connections. However, we must also take into account the negative effects of low-quality ones, which are characterized as contractual and weaker on dimensions like as trust, liking, respect and exchange. The findings of our study, along with those of other researchers, indicate that less-favoured subordinates frequently experience feelings of resentment or "relative deprivation" (a term coined by Mark Bolino, a professor at the University of Oklahoma), which can lead to behaviours such as active mistrust, hate, disdain and avoidance. As a result, they are unable to engage in productive teamwork, team problem-solving, information sharing and discretionary effort, which further solidifies their status as members of an out-group.

This dilemma is brought to light by a longitudinal study that we carried out in collaboration with a global insurer. Executives were provided with input from all of their direct reports prior to participating in a large-scale development programme. This feedback was intended to assist executives in identifying areas in which they could improve. Following that, the leaders were provided with individualized training, one-on-one coaching and peer mentoring at predetermined intervals throughout the course of a year. Following that, the same employees were asked to re-evaluate their managers on the same dimensions. Despite the fact that all of the managers had made clear progress, it did not register uniformly within their respective teams. Subordinates whose initial ratings were one standard deviation below the mean appeared to be the least likely to acknowledge future progress. On the other hand, one may expect the harshest critics to be the first to notice and the most appreciative of change. However, we discovered the exact opposite to be true.

In-group or out-group dynamics can become even more challenging to negotiate as a result of two further rising trends: virtual and hybrid workplaces, as well as the desire to make teams more diverse. These trends raise the likelihood of miscommunication, divides, allegations of bias and feelings of neglect.

Here are three important things that team leaders should take away from this: strained relationships are more common than you might believe. Even if you only sense favouritism, it might have a much higher impact than you might think. Furthermore, the longer these issues remain unreported and unresolved, the more damage they do to the situation.

Attempting to Avoid Conflict

The following are two examples. Léa, an ambitious executive working for a European conglomerate, was hired by the company's chief operating officer (COO) four years ago with the intention of assisting the nine managing directors who manage business units in reorganizing their portfolios and models. The decision was made with the expectation that she would eventually move into one of those jobs. The original assignment that she was given has been extended three times, despite the fact that there has been turnover and promotion among the MDs. Despite this, she continues to feel like an outsider, waiting for her opportunity to manage a unit. There are less opportunities for her to communicate to her employer than there are for her peers, and when they do meet, he is evasive regarding her development path. She shared this information with us. Unbeknownst to her manager, she is dissatisfied with the fact that she is being "strung along," that she has lost trust in the chief operating officer, and that she is contemplating leaving the company.

Aisha, a very skilled pharmaceutical executive who was just recently hired for a high-level role on a worldwide team, is located on a different continent than her manager and colleagues. As a result, she has spent the previous three months participating in team meetings through the use of video conferences. According to what she shared with us, her supervisor does not make much of an attempt to include her in the conversation or to seek her opinion on matters that are not under her purview. He appears to give her less consideration, counsel and encouragement than he does to other members of the team, and he has hardly gotten to know her. In fact, she stated that they have not had a single conversation that is significant to them. "He's just so frustrating," she said, adding that she was already considering resuming her job search, which was still in the process of being considered an option.

The argument is that brilliant and productive employees might easily start to feel like outsiders as a result of neglect or mistakes of omission, such as failing to ask questions of them, listening to them, supporting them, praising them or helping them develop. The majority of the time, leaders are ignorant that anything is wrong for extended periods of time because the behaviours in question do not constitute the transgressions. Additionally, new research conducted by Nikos Dimotakis of Oklahoma State University and colleagues suggests that the quality of relationships between managers and direct reports can change even from week to week. This is something that can occur even within the same week. That is why it is of the utmost importance to do regular assessments of how you are managing everyone and preventing any possible conflicts from occurring.

We recommend that managers begin with a brief audit at the end of each week, which is a natural time period that is long enough to make it representative but short enough to remember the specifics of your numerous encounters. This recommendation is based on the research methodology that the Dimotakis team has developed during their work. You should ask yourself three straightforward questions for each direct report in order to evaluate the quality of your relationship with them. (We recommend using straightforward yes-or-no responses in order to circumvent responses that are self-serving or socially desirable.)

1. Have you attempted to find the person's company? Did your conversations go beyond the tasks that were immediately assigned to you in order to talk about matters that are more general or to engage in social conversation?
2. Have you taken into account the capabilities of the individual? During meetings, did you solicit feedback (opinions and suggestions) from the subordinates, or did you give more weight to their ideas?
3. A person's development was aided by your presence. Did you make a contribution to learning and growth by your words or actions, such as by completing challenging assignments, receiving coaching or providing constructive feedback?

In the event that even one of these questions is answered with a negative response, and especially if this occurs for two or three weeks in a row, you are required to address the deficit. If you want to create a stronger rapport with someone, you should go out to them and find areas of common ground that you might have ignored, such as children, hobbies or upbringing. There is a substantial correlation between perceived resemblance and like. In order to make your employees feel more capable, you should solicit their ideas and proposals and provide them with the opportunity to solve problems in their own unique way. Recognize their competence and what they have accomplished, and be willing to accept reasons if they do not perform up to expectations. Their career goals should be discussed, and they should be given demanding duties, opportunities for advancement and public acclaim for their achievements in order to encourage progress.

Attempting to Mend a Relationship

When leaders fail to handle their out-groups in an acceptable manner, members of the group can grow so frustrated that they reach a point where they are unwilling to overlook the situation. A striking illustration of that occurred not too long ago. The information that one of Hashim's direct subordinates, Stefan, was speaking negatively about him behind his back was brought to Hashim's attention by a colleague at an investment bank. According to Hashim's recollection, "He would sit quietly during meetings and saying nothing." He came to the realization that this was a component of his failure; he was treating Stefan differently than he treated the other members of his team because he did not have the same chemistry with Stefan as he did with the other members! "I probably wasn't paying enough attention or asking myself how he was doing," Hashim admitted. He made the decision to set the record straight.

On the other hand, when he approached Stefan to discuss the issue, he almost immediately received a negative response. Hashim claims that his subordinate informed him directly, "There is no way I can work with you. And by the way, I'm interviewing for a new job." Stefan was not selected for the assignment, and Hashim was unable to fire him because his performance was still satisfactory.

In circumstances such as these, even when it appears that the relationship is irreparable, you have the ability to moderate the negative feelings of your employee and maybe turn the situation around. Our advice is to take three steps.

1. You should get ready for the conversation. It may be beneficial to engage in role-playing with a coach, a reliable colleague or even just an empty chair. You should just picture the member of the team who is dissatisfied with being on the out-group and then have a conversation with that individual, sharing your ideas and feelings regarding how you relate to each other. By doing so, you will be able to articulate your perspectives on the connection, which will assist you in releasing any unpleasant feelings. After that, go through the motions of physically switching places, act as if you are the employee and answer to what you just stated from that point of view. You can continue this fictitious conversation through a number of rounds in order to provide yourself with the opportunity to gain new perspectives on the thinking of both parties in a risk-free manner, to comprehend the role that you play in the issue, to acquire a more realistic understanding of how the conversation might progress and to assist in the development of empathy for your subordinate. When executives have challenged their own convictions and causal attributions before to an actual talk, we have discovered that they are more attentive to the messages that their counterparts have to provide during the actual discussion.

2. Take part. In order to establish a setting in which sceptical subordinates have the impression that they can safely discuss the suffering they experience as a member of an out-group, supervisors must first reduce

the power difference. It is beneficial to meet on neutral ground and to establish the tone by expressly accepting the employee's right to see things differently, to dispute and to disagree, as well as your own responsibility for enabling an unhappy dynamic to spin out of control. In order to get the conversation started, you could say something along the lines of, "I've been thinking about my working relationships with the members of our team today." Following that, we suggest that you consult the practical advise on tough talks that is provided by Douglas Stone, Bruce Patton and Sheila Heen of Harvard Law School. Engage in a "learning conversation" by bringing to the surface and sorting out your own perspectives on what has occurred, the impact it has had on each of you, the contributions you have made, how you feel about the situation and how it affects your identities. Prompts such as "How do you see it?" are helpful examples. I would like to hear more about the reasons why you find this to be essential, as well as what we could have done differently.

3. Form a strategy. The expertise that we have gained when coaching elite teams has shown us that a good method for a superior and a subordinate to begin the process of reestablishing trust is to first articulate what is important to each individual and then commit to making changes. That not only provides a sense of joint accountability but also sends a message that you have good intentions, demonstrates that you want to draw your subordinate closer to you and affirms that you want to bring them closer to you. It is imperative that this plan be produced through a process that is equitable, that it incorporates creative choices and that

it has a realistic end point. It is not the purpose to become friends with the subordinate; rather, it is to repair a relationship that is productive and respectful, one in which you can work together towards a similar professional or organizational goal, even if that goal includes making the subordinate's transition to another team easier.

One That Is in Your Favour

In spite of the fact that managers and dissatisfied employees from out-groups rarely adhere to a formal code of conduct, the following is an example of how they may establish fundamental guidelines.

Aiming for Yourself

"I am counting on you to produce outcomes that can be relied upon in order to make progress with our team."

"I ask that you refrain from criticism of me behind my back."

"I am in need of your active support as I prepare for the next step in my professional life."

"For the purpose of honing my talents, I require access to chances for professional growth or training."

The Interaction

"Speak out early if a task appears to be unclear or if you encounter challenges that were not anticipated."

"When we get to a decision about what course of action to take, kindly execute it."

"I will feel less pressure to check on you if you keep me continuously updated on the progress that has been made."

"Let's rely on data to guide our conversations rather than relying solely on our sentiments or opinions."

"When you observe an unexpected event, you should refrain from making hasty judgements about my judgement or my level of expertise. Be sure to look into what took place."

"Please give me the opportunity to present a solution before you start coming up with suggestions."

"Give me a say in the amount of monitoring I receive and the kind of monitoring that is most effective for me."

The Pet Peeves

"Please do not surprise me in any way. Please let me know if you are going to miss any important deadlines or deliverables."

"I don't anticipate that you will be checking your email at all hours of the day or night, but I do anticipate that you will respond in a timely manner."

"My request is that you refrain from asking me questions to which you already know the answers."

"To avoid confusion, please differentiate between suggestions and orders."

Disconflict

"If we are in disagreement, let us not bring up the past but rather remain in the here and now."

"In the event that we have a significant disagreement, let us invite a mediator to assist us in working through the issue."

Hashim and Stefan were able to reach a consensus through a series of conversations that were led by Hashim. The agreement stipulated that Stefan would refrain from complaining and would continue to do his duties, while Hashim would assist Stefan in locating prospects for internal transfer. The result was more harm limiting than damage restoration, although it was still beneficial. A disruptive subordinate was neutralized by Hashim, which brought to an improvement in team spirit and safeguarded his reputation.

It is common for managers to fail to recognize the existence of out-groups since they receive positive feedback from their in-groups and are aware that they are not considered to be "bad" bosses. The costs, however, might be significant if any employee is allowed to feel disregarded. Because of this, it is of the utmost importance to recognize when the dynamics of the team feel uneven, to prevent conflicts from occurring and to make an effort to repair any harm that has already been done. A tremendous opportunity lies in acquiring the skills necessary to properly manage your out-group. Increases in consideration, coaching and appreciation, even if they are quite minor, have the potential to improve productivity, well-being and cohesiveness.

6

Hey CEO, What's Your Leadership Style?

There is a great deal of literature that discusses the many leadership styles that are prevalent and how to choose which type is most suitable for you, whether it be transactional or transformational, bureaucratic or laissez-faire leaders. On the other hand, Daniel Goleman, a psychologist who is most recognized for his work on emotional intelligence, asserts that "being a great leader means recognizing that different circumstances may call for different approaches."

Goleman has discovered six distinct leadership styles that managers can adjust to, based on the circumstances and the requirements of their team members. He has derived these styles from study and experience. These leadership styles were initially presented by him in his article titled "Leadership That Gets Results," which was published in the *Harvard Business Review* in 2000. Since then, they have gained widespread recognition as a necessary framework for effective leadership. Among the six different types of leadership are:

- A style of leadership known as coercive, which involves demanding rapid cooperation from followers.
- A leadership style known as authoritative leadership, which focuses on inciting individuals to work towards a common goal.

- A leadership style known as pacesetting, which emphasizes self-direction and the expectation of doing excellent work.
- An affiliation-based leadership style, which places an emphasis on the formation of emotional connections.
- The democratic style of leadership, which entails the process of reaching a consensus.
- A leadership style known as coaching, which places an emphasis on the development of individuals for the future.

Despite the fact that the world has evolved over the course of the previous twenty years, these leadership styles continue to be applicable. If you are able to master them, you will be able to negotiate the intricacies of many circumstances, increase morale and promote the long-term growth of your team.

With this in mind, let's take a more in-depth look at each of the six different leadership styles, as well as the appropriate times to employ each one, in light of the current state of the corporate world.

1. **Coercive Leadership Style:** According to the research conducted by Goleman, the most ineffective form of leadership is the coercive approach in the majority of instances. It is not hard to comprehend the reason behind this. He claims that this style is characterized by decisions being made from the top down, an authoritarian approach and a demanding attitude that is characterized by doing what I say. Despite the fact that this approach might produce results in the short term, it has a detrimental effect on the culture of the firm over the long run, resulting in a high employee turnover rate as well as a staff that is disillusioned and disengaged.

When it is appropriate to employ the coercive leadership style? It is possible that this command-and-control style of leadership could be effective in specific crisis scenarios that require prompt, decisive action and a clear chain of command. For example, a corporate takeover or an emergency room are two examples of such situations. However, according to Goleman, this strategy is likely to be counterproductive in the majority of situations.

2. **Authoritative Leadership Style:** It is important to note that the authoritative leadership style is not to be mistaken with the authoritarian leadership style. This type of leadership entails inspiring your team members by connecting their work to a bigger organizational strategy. This means assisting them in comprehending how their day-to-day activities contribute to a wider cause. This is not about micromanaging; rather, it is about creating clear guidelines. High levels of employee engagement and enhanced job satisfaction are the results of allowing your staff members to work towards the common goal with autonomy and creativity. This is necessary in order to achieve the desired results. If authoritative leadership is the most effective and inspiring form of leadership, then coercive leadership appears to be the worst kind of leadership.

When it is appropriate to utilize the authoritative managerial style? The leadership style in question is advantageous in a wide variety of circumstances, but it is especially helpful during periods of transition or without assurance. Furthermore, it is possible to incorporate it into day-to-day operations by bringing to the attention of your team members the objective of your organization in a natural way. A manager in the pharmaceutical industry may say something like, "Our work will benefit many patients," whereas a leader in the insurance industry might say something like, "We are helping people secure their livelihood." The staff is able to better understand the organization's goals and mission as a result of these reminders, which make them more concrete.

3. **Pacesetting Leadership Style:** Holding yourself and others to high standards is an essential component of this effective leadership style. It is commendable to strive for perfection; nevertheless, the pacesetting method is counterproductive if the emphasis is placed on shortcomings rather than triumphs of the organization. According to Goleman, the persistent desire for productivity and results can also result in the creation of a work environment that is a pressure cooker.

    The excessive emphasis placed on perfection can also make it difficult for employees to understand how their individual efforts fit into the greater plan, which can result in an increase in employee turnover.

    How to know when to apply the leadership style that sets the pace? While it is recommended that this approach be utilized infrequently, it is possible for it to be successful in certain situations, particularly when your personnel are extremely driven and exceptionally talented. One example of a group that might benefit from it is research and development or legal teams. Even in these circumstances, however, it is essential to strike a balance between setting the pace and alternative ways in order to minimize consequences such as staff burnout.

4. **Affiliative Leadership Style:** The development of strong emotional relationships, the establishment of a sense of camaraderie and team spirit, and the promotion of a good and supportive work environment are all components of this type of leadership. The members of the team are able to feel like they belong, openly share their ideas and opinions

and collaborate with one another to achieve common goals as a result of this.

According to Goleman, this relationship-oriented style is particularly useful in the process of building a happy work environment. This is of utmost significance at a time when some businesses are requesting that their employees return to the office. According to him, if you take the time to get to know your employees on a personal level and celebrate their successes, you can transform your workplace into a community that is more compassionate and cohesive than an administrative machine.

When it is appropriate to employ the affiliative leadership style? Despite the fact that this approach fosters excellent business culture and leads to the formation of connections, it should not be utilized in isolation. In order to fix performance concerns or deal with complex challenges, it is possible that it does not provide appropriate feedback. It is possible to achieve a greater sense of equilibrium by combining this technique with the authoritative and inspirational style, which provides both support and guidance.

5. **Democratic Leadership Style:** Providing your team with the opportunity to participate in decision-making is an essential component of the democratic leadership style. You demonstrate to the members of your team that their opinions are being taken into consideration, that their voices are being heard and that their efforts are being respected by taking the time to collect input, listen to concerns and varied perspectives, and incorporate comments. Their sense of ownership and duty is increased as a result of this.

How to know when to adopt the democratic style of leadership? This approach is perfect for situations in which you are unsure of the most effective way to proceed and that you want to produce ideas. However, it is not a suitable method to use when the members of your team do not have sufficient expertise or information, or when there is a crisis.

6. **Coaching Leadership Style:** The coaching method places an emphasis on the development of the individual and requires you to devote some of your time to gaining an understanding of the long-term objectives of your team members, which may include both their personal and professional progress. "Asking questions such as, 'What do you want from your life, your career, and this job?'" According to Goleman, asking your staff, "And, how can I help you?" inspires people to think about their goals and strive towards achieving them. Employees are more likely to feel valued and motivated when they are given the opportunity to participate in their own professional growth.

   How to know when to employ the coaching style of leadership? According to him, this manner of communication is particularly helpful when doing one-on-one performance evaluations; but, it may also be included into ordinary interactions. It is possible for a leader who is in the coach mode to remark something like, "You are very good at XYZ, but when you do ABC, it does not work as well because of these reasons." To what extent have you thought about attempting this alternative method instead? Instead of allowing potential issues to fester, this real-time feedback helps staff develop and learn; it prevents problems from lingering.

It has been found that the most successful leaders are able to modify their approach to suit the specific circumstances at hand, whether it be a change in the environment, a modification in the dynamics of the organization or a change in the business cycle. As a result, it is essential that you maintain a heightened awareness of your surroundings, comprehend the influence that you have on other people and adapt your strategy accordingly. The most effective leaders are able to move between several leadership styles according to the circumstances.

As it appears in the real world, altering styles looks like this: you would employ an authoritative approach when beginning a new project, which is necessary in situations when there is a need for clear direction and a compelling vision in order to pull the team together and encourage everyone to work towards a common objective. In situations where an employee is having difficulty with a certain work and you need to assist them in learning a new ability, you would transition to a coaching style of management. In addition, you would use a pacesetting technique when your team of employees, who are both dedicated and experienced, is tasked with meeting a deadline that is particularly difficult.

If, on the other hand, you believe that you lack the capabilities necessary to adopt a fresh and distinct leadership style, let alone more than one, what would you do?

According to Goleman, all individuals have the ability to broaden their range of leadership styles via the application of committed effort and repetition. In addition to this, he suggests that you concentrate on developing your emotional intelligence. According to what he writes in his essay for the *Harvard Business Review* from the year 2000, "In order to broaden [their style repertoires], leaders must first understand which emotional intelligence competencies underlie the leadership styles they are lacking." It is then possible for them to work diligently in order to enhance their quotient of them. As an illustration, an affiliative leader possesses strengths in three different emotional intelligence domains, including empathy, the ability to form relationships and communication. Such guidance regarding the addition of capacities may appear to be overly simplistic, such as "go change yourself," yet it is fully possible to improve one's emotional intelligence via practice.

There is some good news: personality is not a predetermined outcome. Even if you are inherently introverted or if you have a tendency to be driven by statistics and analysis rather than emotion, you can still learn how to adapt diverse leadership styles in order to organize, motivate and guide your team.

According to the research of Daniel Goleman, "the success of a leader is dependent on the productivity and effectiveness of the people who work for them." According to him, "If you use a style of leadership that is counterproductive to their performance, you are shooting yourself in the foot."

7

Making Sense of the CEO's Management Style

W.C.H. Prentice's 1961 article "Understanding Leadership" in the *Harvard Business Review* disapproving of leadership being defined by control and authority or exceptional analytical prowess laid the groundwork for many of the ideas advanced by more contemporary writers like Abraham Zaleznik and Daniel Goleman, who have reshaped our understanding of leadership in profound ways. According to Prentice, leadership is "the accomplishment of a goal through the direction of human assistants." An effective leader is someone who can read the room, identify the drivers of employee behaviour and rally the troops in a way that serves the greater good while also satisfying workers' unique passions and requirements. Without instituting anarchy, he argued for democratic leadership that provides workers with chances to learn and advance. Although Prentice's terminology is a bit rudimentary at times, his insights on how CEOs may inspire their teams to rally around the company's objectives are both relevant and ahead of their time.

When someone tries to analyse leadership, they usually end up failing because they have the wrong idea of what they're trying to do. Leadership is something he rarely, if ever, studies. On the contrary, he delves into the realms of charisma, influence, performance and strategic foresight. These are nice to haves for some leaders, but they don't make them great leaders.

Leadership entails guiding a group of people to achieve a common objective. Leadership is the art of getting people to work together towards a common goal. An exceptional leader is one who maintains their composure under pressure year after year, no matter how diverse the challenges.

No amount of power, intimidation or the threat of physical damage may ever be used by him in any of his transactions. His admirers and followers may never submit to his every whim, and he may never enjoy widespread popularity. His leadership and the group's goals will remain under the radar unless he adopts some striking personality traits. In terms of the crucial issue of goal-setting, he might not be very skilled or influential; in his role as leader, he might just be a go-getter.

He has succeeded in a way no one else has because he has taken the time to learn about his coworkers and how their individual objectives relate to the collective objective that he must accomplish.

Difficulties and Delusions

Concisely describing the actions of effective leaders is not difficult. However, isolating the factors that dictate their performance is a considerably more daunting task. It is common practice to adequately identify each worker's role so that he can anticipate the fulfilment of a significant interest or motivation of his in the execution of the group enterprise. A crude style of leadership is one that is based on a reliance on material gains or the eradication of anxieties about different types of insecurity as the only means of gratification. People do their best to complete the task at hand because they know that if they don't, they risk losing their jobs.

In certain contexts, it's undeniable that these kinds of incentives work. They accomplish this mechanically by tying an employee's interests to those of their company or group. However, the shortcomings of such straightforward methods are obvious to everyone. We humans don't have a single set of controls like a machine. When their multi-faceted reactions to love, status, autonomy, accomplishment and belonging to a group go unnoticed in the workplace, they become, at best, inefficient robots and, at worst, defiant slaves who destroy the very things they are meant to be helping.

It is paradoxical that our default mental image of "the leader" is typically a military commander, given that, for the most part, organizations in the military exemplify the most simplistic usage of positive and negative reinforcement as forms of motivation. World War II's coining of the term "snafu" (situation normal, all fouled up) exemplifies what has been well-documented in military literature from ancient Greece and Rome to the modern era: namely, that no other human endeavour is frequently characterized by such low morale, goldbricking and waste.

To the military's credit, two points stand out:

1. Without a doubt, the military has unique challenges. There are good reasons to treat males mechanically and uniformly since they die and must be replaced.
2. Having a clear understanding of who is responsible for what, as is fostered by an authoritarian command structure, is crucial in any group endeavour, but especially in combat. Some people still think anarchy exists wherever there is a leadership style that is not fundamentally military.

Everyone has heard the saying "somebody's got to be the boss," and I doubt many would argue with that. However, one must exercise caution when equating the organizational structure or line of command with a means of accomplishing tasks. Comparable instead to a football play diagram, which depicts both the overall strategy and the specific ways in which each player is involved.

There is no leadership in the diagram. On its own, it doesn't indicate anything about the play's execution. However, the issue of leadership is just this: how to effectively execute. While incentives and punishments can get the job done, in the end, everyone has to know their role and how it fits into the bigger picture if the team is going to continue to succeed and keep morale high. Making these desires a reality and figuring out how to direct current desires into productive collaboration is a challenge for any leader.

Personal Connections

When the leader achieves success, it will be due to his understanding of two fundamental truths: people are diverse and complex. In addition to the classic donkey-and-carrot combination, there are countless other aspects and patterns of emotion and thinking that define men, such as ambition, patriotism, love of the good and beautiful, boredom, self-doubt and countless more. However, not every employee has the same hobbies, and not every employee's employment allows him to fully satisfy all of his interests. To illustrate:

- A guy's everyday work may have little to do with his profound religious desire, even yet it may be the defining characteristic of that personality.

- Someone else might get a rush out of solving complex issues, but he might never see the practical applications of his interests in chess and mathematics in his work.
- Yet another may be perpetually irritated since his boss never seems to notice or capitalize on his need for a pleasant, adoring relationship, which he is severely lacking at home.

If the leader is in a position to respond to these unique patterns, he will have a better chance of inspiring followers to care deeply about the task at hand—if his abilities and circumstances allow it. Finally, in an ideal company, employees at all levels report to a single boss whose sphere of influence is just small enough for him to get to know his subordinates on a personal level.

When the Golden Rule Doesn't Apply

Thankfully, there are some universally effective norms of motivation, and the primary motives of persons in the same society are frequently quite similar. One notable example is the renowned prescriptions in *How to Win Friends and Influence People* by Dale Carnegie, which have proven to be effective. Its central tenet is an adaptation of the golden rule: treat others as you would like to be treated. Although simplistic and severely lacking in detail, this rule represents a significant advance over the previous methods of coercion and the direct method of rewarding desirable actions.

The treat others as you would be treated school of thought produces some of the most ineffectual leaders in the world, and it would be a huge error to ignore this. We have all met selfless people who meant well and tried their best to help others, but who failed miserably in executive roles (or even friendships or marriages) because they failed to recognize that people's preferences and emotional needs were unique from their own. Everyone is familiar with certain types of people: those who work nonstop and never seem to tyre or get bored, those who love to tell stories in bars and think it's funny to do it even to women, those who are passionate about public service and try to influence others by giving them free tickets to lectures about African mission work, those who are miserly and believe that everyone is after money, and so on.

An exceptional leader's ability to comprehend his coworkers is the source of his one-of-a-kind human and social accomplishment. A leader must be more astute and nuanced than the adage "do as you would be done by" suggests.

Whoever leads us well must appear to comprehend our aims and objectives. He has to look like he can meet their needs, that he knows what he's doing and how it will affect others, and that he's consistent and unambiguous when making decisions. "Seem" is a key word in this context. It won't matter how competent the would-be leader is if we don't see him as having these qualities. We are committed to not following his lead. However, we will continue to follow him until we realize our mistake if we have been deceived and he just appears to possess these qualities. What this means is that his ability to influence his followers is highly dependent on the impression he makes at any given moment.

Fallacies in Viewing

Recognizing their leader for who he truly is could be just as challenging for followers as it is for leaders to fully comprehend each other. Misunderstandings between supervisors and subordinates are a common source of tension in the workplace.

The assumptions and biases we bring to bear on the world shape our perceptions of it. The facts could not seem the same to my boss or employer since my perception of him is influenced by my assumptions of how other bosses act. Poor leadership is often the result of either the subordinate's oversimplification of the situation or the superior's inability to understand the subordinate's perspective.

For instance, an employee may see a promotion offer as a threat since it takes them away from the security of their guaranteed, albeit gradual, advancement in the company. No matter how helpful it is for improving efficiency, a shift in reporting or authority structures may be perceived as an attack on one's dignity. Some may worry that their employment is in jeopardy due to the implementation of a technique that saves labour. Someone might see an invitation to talk about corporate policy as a sophisticated trap to get them to confess to having heretical or disloyal opinions. The introduction of a new fringe perk could be seen as a justification for not increasing compensation. Thus, every level of staff should report to a single boss whose territory is just small enough for him to get to know his subordinates on a personal level in an ideal workplace.

The boss is usually unprepared for these interpretations, which make them seem foolish, deceitful or even twisted. The effective leader, however, will have anticipated and planned for such reactions. He must have been aware that a large portion of his staff has been socialized to view their bosses as inherent adversaries; as a result, it is instinctive for them to "act like an employee" in this regard and to be wary of seemingly amicable attempts at conciliation from above.

There is an equally terrible flip side to the same problem. Acting superior to others is not only ineffective, but also harmful. For example, many bosses are resistant to new ideas in industrial relations because they believe these principles would undermine their long-held image as corporate dictators. Their reputation hinders labour relations growth.

Difficulties Faced by an Underling

However, effective business executives will be able to identify and address a different, more nuanced element that may mediate between employers and employees. Being a subordinate is psychologically challenging, and that is a factor. Being a subordinate is not an easy job. Taking commands from someone else restricts my ability to make my own decisions and use my own judgement; it sets boundaries within which I am more likely to comply with his wants than my own. In order to embrace this position without resistance or friction, I need to either discover that the balance between reliance and independence is exactly what I need or see it as a reflection of an order that transcends my own specific circumstances (such as my age, class, rank, etc.). The real-world effects of these two options are distinct.

One reason is that it's more challenging to follow instructions from someone I don't see as superior. A tragic example of ineffective practical leadership could be an executive who tries too hard to blend in with the crew, destroying any respect or admiration his employees may have had for him. As a result, they start to see him as just another guy, and they start to question why they should follow his orders. A compassionate boss won't show his employees that he thinks they're stupid, but he should probably keep his distance psychologically so they can accept his authority without animosity.

At least occasionally, the goals of the subordinate will be frustrated when one of two individuals in a superior position has to make the final call. Aggression ensues as a result of frustration. In other words, resisting is an innate human response to being obstructed. It takes little training to develop the habit of being prepared to fight or defend oneself in dealing with the boss.

The situation becomes even more problematic when the work environment discourages expressing anger towards the employer. This can lead to a vicious cycle where employees respond to dissatisfaction by becoming even more irritated. The hardships of being an employee can spark daily animosity, which can be exacerbated by devices like suggestion boxes, grievance panels and departmental rivalries. To keep the unavoidable psychological repercussions of following commands from becoming too overwhelming, a good leader will know that there needs to be a balance between reliance and independence, restraint, and autonomy.

The best part is that he'll see that a lot of people are scared of being totally independent and would rather have some rules that restrict their freedom. He will make an effort to cater his subordinates' psychological demands by adjusting the levels and types of freedom they are given. Typically, this entails offering a growth programme that gives the employee a clear picture of his future with the company, while a good leader will ensure that the picture is grounded in reality. This is where a comparison could be useful.

The kind of fake democracy that exists in certain households is the single most effective way to bring morale crashing down in any group setting. Even parents who promise their kids equal say in every choice eventually realize they can't keep it up, and the kids feel especially left out when the plan backfires. All of the decisions that aren't made through voting or consultation, which happens frequently, start to seem arbitrary to them. A sense of unfairness and rebellion is deeply ingrained in them.

Many employees have been socialized to view their employers negatively, and a good leader understands this.

In business, too, these things are true. Pretending that subordinates can make decisions when they cannot accomplish anything is pointless. If you want your subordinate to be able to make decisions or at least have input on those that fall under their purview, you need to establish clear boundaries between their authority and yours. After you've drawn those lines, you can't cross them more frequently than is absolutely required.

The ideal working environment for a subordinate is one in which he can go about his business unsupervised. The subordinate should be empowered to make the required decisions, while the superior should provide clarification on the goals and potential alternatives to accomplishing them. Even if autocrats from "the old school" give that ideal lip service, it won't mean anything if it sounds false. The employee will not take a chance on plan B, which could lead to the loss of his job, if he knows that plan A is preferred by the boss. He can only play it safe by aligning himself with his superior's opinions in every instance if he is aware that his job is dependent on every significant choice. But now he's just another mindless cog in the machine that can't think for himself or relieve his bosses of decision-making duties. Nobody respects him, not even his own boss, who had a hand in shaping him that way.

Developmental Objectives

Unless there is a consideration of potential benefits and drawbacks, the decision is not worthwhile. A man's opinion would not be necessary if it were certain. We all make mistakes. Rather than expecting employees to never make a mistake, we should demand that they reflect on and improve upon their past actions. It is the executive's responsibility to track his team's development over time and make sure that, as they gain experience, their triumphs surpass their setbacks.

An essential component of lasting leadership is this idea of long-term growth. It is important for every man to understand that his position within the group might grow and change based on what he does. In particular, he has to perceive the leader as the guy who cares about his development and is willing to lend a hand. Having interested staff members or personnel officers who do not participate in policymaking is insufficient. No matter how much technical help they provide, they will never be able to replace the interest of the accountable executive.

Handling Polite

Exactly at this moment are misunderstandings frequently discovered. It is unreasonable to expect an executive to fill in for a parent, a psychiatrist, or even the head of staff. His interest should not be biased or personal in the least. This is how he might approach the employee:

"This is not an intimate matter. The treatment would be uniform for everyone in your position. However, I will ensure that you are given every opportunity to showcase your full ability for the duration of your employment with me. As a part of my role, I ensure your happiness and progress. My opinion of this company will improve in direct proportion to how quickly you become a key player here. Come talk to me about what's holding you back if you notice a better method to complete your work. You may count on my undivided attention and assistance, as well as the accolades you rightfully deserve, if you are correct."

A worker can't improve in a meaningful way until they learn. At regular intervals, the superior should reflect on the accomplishments and setbacks, and ensure that the subordinate shares his perspective on these events and their outcomes. A very challenging facet of leadership becomes apparent at this stage of evaluation. In what ways might objective criticism be effective? How may one criticize a decision or a practise without making the worker feel personally degraded?

There are two reasons why good communication is crucial now. Employee morale might take a hit in the long run, and in the near term, the employee might not put out his best effort to implement the boss's alternative plan for fear that his decision was correct. By approaching a situation coldly and ignoring the human emotions and motivations at play, it is all too simple for a leader to incite hostility and defensiveness.

We may reasonably question if we have not tended to separate management conduct from behaviour outside of the office—in the family, for example—because such failures appear to occur more frequently in office settings than anywhere else. Getting our wants granted at home via a formal document like a letter or order is not something we take for granted. A key life skill for most average-IQ individuals is learning to influence people to do what they want them to. Establishing an appropriate emotional and personal context that is suitable for the one making the request (whether it a wife, adult son, adolescent daughter or child) is as natural as breathing.

At work, we pretend to be an executive or boss and set aside our natural abilities in dealing with people.

We also probably know how to tailor a vacation package to appeal to different family members' interests—for example, a wife who likes to be served, a son who wants to go fishing, or a daughter who wants to spend time with friends her own age. Also, we might find out that one of them is more amenable to compromise if she is involved in making decisions, while the other prefers to have things handed to him in a prefabricated form. When we're at home, we likely don't give much consideration to how to respond to such discrepancies.

When we're at work, though, we put on our executive or employer hats and put our everyday intuitive abilities in dealing with people on ice. In our haste to get things done, we issue cold, impersonal commands to whomever is in charge of carrying them out, completely ignoring the fact that everyone's cooperation is essential for a successful mobilization of human resources. Interactions between individuals constitute leadership. To pull it off, you need a leader who can tap into the unique qualities and abilities of your followers.

Methods Used by a Master Conductor of Symphonies

Some of the key relationships that exist in every leadership scenario can be learned from an orchestra director:

1. The idea that the men need to be well-trained and equipped for their jobs is obvious in this context, yet it's easy to forget. It is not always the boss's fault when a group fails. A high school band will not able to provide Toscanini with high-quality music.
2. In order to complete the shared objective, a psychological environment must be created. The logistics of beginning rehearsal should not get in the way of the musical goal; hence, it is important for a conductor to establish ground rules, signals and personal preferences in such a way. Every workplace needs well-defined norms that everyone can get behind, just like a conductor needs a set of

ground rules for rehearsal. Punctuality, smoking and talking in between numbers, new versus old music, and a host of other issues could derail his team's progress towards their goal.

3. First and foremost, the musicians need to feel that they have contributed to the creation of music that their leader is proud of. His leadership will be ineffective and his music will be subpar until each member finds personal satisfaction. While some illustrious conductors have ruled over their musicians like petty dictators, others have been godfathers to their own children and played poker with them. To a large extent, these things don't matter. The great conductor succeeds in making every instrumentalist feel as though he is contributing to the creation of unique music. Characteristics and habits of an individual may play a supporting role, serving to reassert and strengthen the crucial representation of a guy who adheres to the utmost musical standards. However, one cannot become a Toscanini simply by mimicking his behaviour.

Leadership with Minimal Stress

These basic realities are frequently disregarded. There is no shortage of leaders in business who only strive to imitate the outward traits of a more successful coworker or boss, failing to inspire their own teams to actively participate by demonstrating how they can find personal fulfilment in the collective effort.

That many companies' finance, manufacturing and research departments view salespeople as an evil necessity and would recoil in horror at the idea of introducing what they perceive as a "sales approach" into management is noteworthy, in my opinion, because it reflects the attitude that these executives adopt. An air of deceit and manipulation permeates some forms of advertising, marketing and sales, which may or may not be the exact cause for it. Even though they know or think that the customer will live to regret the purchase, the salespeople and advertising I'm referring to are frequently eager to find and exploit a customer's vulnerability in order to close the deal.

Though they may get you what you want in the short term, manipulative social and psychological tactics have no place in a long-term partnership. Every good salesperson knows that in a perfect world, both parties should come out ahead in a business deal. And it involves listening to the consumer, clarifying his demands so he can understand them, and then delivering a product that fits the bill. If a salesperson is properly trained in this method, they will be an exceptional executive who seamlessly transitions from sales to administrative interactions.

On the other hand, the cunning, fast-talking con artist who takes delight in outwitting his clients—the kind who can sell cigarettes to men by appealing to their vanity or cosmetics to women by appealing to their ambition—may eventually become an executive who treats his employees with the same disdain he did his clients. If he takes pleasure in manipulating his employees by appealing to their emotions and desires, they will eventually catch on and the trust and devotion that are crucial for good leadership will be eroded.

When all else fails, a CEO must draw on his people skills and knowledge to achieve what an orchestra conductor does: bring subordinates joy through their work for the greater good. Nothing in all those charming displays of charm and charisma will be able to satisfy him.

Despite popular belief, leadership is about much more than simply pushing other people around, being nice to people or understanding people. Some people mistakenly believe that in a democratic society, there is no division of power and that everyone may be their own boss. That is completely absurd, particularly in a corporate context. Leadership in business, however, can be democratic if it maximizes employees' opportunities for advancement without allowing chaos to ensue.

Before a leader can reach his full potential, he must ensure that functions are organized and that his position is well understood within that framework. It is the responsibility of a leader to ensure that everyone in the group knows their specific duty and how to contribute to the greater good so that everyone can achieve their deepest desires.

8

From Good to Great CEO

In general, things follow a continuous pattern. From money (poor to comfortable to rich) to temperature (cold to hot with tepid in the midst), we rank everything. The inescapable laws of hydrodynamics provide a linear continuity that aids in understanding the complexity of society and science and has the potential for advancement and development.

On the other hand, it would be easy to assume that there is a spectrum for leadership qualities, with excellent leadership occupying the middle ground. There is a long-held conviction that leadership is structured in a predictable way, and that one can rise up the ranks by accumulating experience and working hard.

There is no doubt that anyone can grow into a leadership role. The unwavering conviction that excellence and goodness are tributaries of one and the same river is what I disagree with. This is completely false. There is a world of difference between excellent leadership and great leadership. There are several facets to leadership. It may be excellent and wonderful, or just one of those things, or neither of them.

The most common openings for the adjective "great" are "to great effect" or "a great effort," both of which imply an exceptionally forceful or intense quality. Although "excellent" is another common meaning of great, it is not its main one. Regarding the term "good," it is typically used to describe morality, virtue and ethics; for example, "a good person" or "a good decision." Good can also mean the quality of something, as opposed to its generally known antonym, evil, but in this case, it means the direction in which behaviour is dictated.

Inspiring, commanding, and frequently overpowering are qualities of great leaders. Its animation alone is enough to captivate viewers. Excellent leadership motivates, inspires and captivates. It's an impassioned plea, shaking people out of their slumber and into action. As one of the strongest forces in human history, it is responsible for both the joys and tragedies that our species has experienced. The people in charge have a great deal of influence over its course, yet it does spark enthusiasm and mobilize groups to action.

To be a good leader is to safeguard and advance generally acknowledged ideals by putting them into practice. As a noun, it means acting morally. While there may be valid disagreements about good and wrong, the universally accepted norms of behaviour that have enabled societies and individuals to prosper over the ages are strikingly consistent. A good person looks out for other people's interests and welfare.

Great leadership is more captivating than good leadership. When goodness prevails, it's hard to tell since everything is going according to plan. In contrast to the dramatic nature of great, good serves as a blended backdrop, a screen built on values, upon which great deeds transpire. For this reason, the direction of good is frequently overshadowed by the force of great.

Great and decent leadership are in a constant and ever-changing tug of war. A tremendous power exists, one that is frequently puzzling, sometimes unreasonable and, most significantly, sometimes uncontrollable. Then, there is good, which is a true north star that points to the values of mutual benefit. Whereas the latter aspirations, the former moves.

The traditional view of leadership as a continuum is common. But that would be to miss the mark on what constitutes excellent leadership. They're totally distinct from one another. It seems irrational to separate them and disrupt the handy continuous. However, it is critical in order to comprehend the factors that account for the functioning and influence of leadership. Good might be sympathetic but powerless, while great can be crucial but destructive. The greatest hope for leadership is for the two to live in harmony; we should be afraid of evil if it exists. To avoid getting stuck, lost, or worse, organizations must find a way to work around the inherent tension between direction and force.

The Actual Role of Leaders

Expanding upon and delving further into the ideas presented in the 1977 essay, "What Leaders Really Do" was initially published in 1990. John Kotter, a former professor at Harvard Business School, has an innovative (and, once articulated, seemingly obvious) theory: management and leadership are distinct but complimentary roles, and, in a dynamic and unpredictable world, neither can succeed without the other. The important roles of a manager and a leader are thereafter listed and compared. His main argument needs restating: in times of uncertainty, only organizations that accept and even embrace the opposing views of stability and change will survive.

Contrary to popular belief, leadership is distinct from management. There is nothing esoteric or mystical about leadership. Having "charisma" or any other unusual personality traits is completely irrelevant. No select few should be entrusted with it. Leadership, on the other hand, is not always an improvement over or substitute for management.

Administration and leadership, on the other hand, are two separate yet complimentary philosophies. Every one of them serves a unique purpose and engages in unique behaviours. To thrive in today's complicated and unpredictable corporate world, you need both.

These days, most American companies are both over-managed and under-led. They ought to work on their ability to lead. When leaders don't materialize, corporations fail. They look for individuals who show signs of having leadership potential and provide them opportunities to grow in their careers. Countless individuals have the potential to assume significant leadership roles within an organization when they are hand-picked, developed and supported.

Companies should keep in mind that having great leaders but ineffective managers is just as bad, if not worse, as the other way around when they work to improve their leadership skills. Finding a happy medium between effective leadership and management is the true test.

The ability to effectively lead and manage is, of course, not innate in every person. Though they may lack the necessary leadership qualities, some individuals have the potential to flourish as managers. Some people are naturally gifted leaders, but they struggle mightily to develop into effective managers for various reasons. Astute businesses recognize the worth of both types of employees and do whatever it takes to integrate them.

Such businesses, however, do the right thing by disregarding the new research that claims humans are incapable of managing and leading when it comes to executive job preparation. Developing leader-managers is their goal. Leadership and management are two very different things, and once businesses grasp this distinction, they can start to prepare their top executives to do both.

Distinguishing Between Leadership and Management

Dealing with complexity is a key component of management. Its methods and practices are mostly a reaction to the rise of huge organizations, which was a major change in the twentieth century. Complex businesses often face extinction-level chaos in the absence of competent management. Important factors, like as product quality and profitability, benefit from a level of order and consistency brought about by competent management.

Leadership, on the other hand, is all about adapting to new circumstances. The increased volatility and intensity of competition in the corporate world in recent years is a contributing factor to its growing significance. Several elements have come together to cause this transition, including increased global competition, deregulation of markets, rapid technical advancement, an unstable oil cartel, raiders using junk bonds, shifting workforce demographics and overcapacity in capital-intensive industries. So, it's no longer enough to just repeat yesterday's actions or improve upon them by five per cent; this is no longer a winning formula. Adapting to this new world and staying competitive requires constant innovation. There must be greater leadership whenever there is more change.

Dealing with complexity is a key component of management. Leadership, on the other hand, is all about adapting to new circumstances.

Take this straightforward military comparison into consideration: during times of peace, an army can typically weather the storm with well-coordinated efforts at all levels of command and a core group of capable commanders at the helm. On the other hand, good leadership is essential for a fighting army. People still need to be led into combat because no one has worked out how to control them successfully.

Management and leadership are defined by the two distinct tasks of dealing with complexity and change. Deciding what needs doing, establishing relationships and networks that can achieve an agenda, and then attempting to get those individuals to actually do it are all parts of every system of action. However, they all manage to get the job done, but in their own unique ways.

The first line of defence against complexity for businesses is careful planning and budgeting. This entails looking forward (usually a month or a year), deciding what the company wants to accomplish and then dividing up the resources needed to make it happen. To the contrary, guiding an organization towards positive transformation starts with charting a course—creating an image of the future (sometimes far off) and plans to bring about the adjustments that will be necessary to get there.

Bringing People Together: Eastman Kodak's Chuck Trowbridge and Bob Crandall

In the early 1970s, Eastman Kodak got into the photocopying industry, specialising in high-tech machines that cost around $60,000 each. The following decade saw this company's revenue nearly triple to $1 billion. However, expenses were substantial, profitability was elusive and issues were pervasive. Kodak lost $40 million in 1984 due to inventory write-offs. Even though most employees were aware of the issues, they were unable to come to a consensus on a solution. Chuck Trowbridge spoke with practically every important person inside his group and with others at Kodak who may have an impact on the copy business in his first two months as general manager of the new copy goods group, which was founded in 1984. Bob Crandall's engineering and manufacturing division was a critical sector.

A less bureaucratic and more decentralized organization was Trowbridge and Crandall's straightforward goal for engineering and manufacturing: to become a world-class manufacturing operation. The message was still hard to get over as it was so different from all that had come before, both inside the copy products business and the rest of Kodak. Crandall instituted a plethora of mechanisms to drive home the new course of action and bring everyone on board with it. These included weekly meetings with his twelve direct reports, monthly "copy product forums" where he would meet with one representative from each of his departments, discussions of new initiatives aimed at improving existing ones, and quarterly "State of the Department" meetings where managers would meet with all of their employees.

At least once a month, Crandall and everyone reporting to him would get together with 80 to 100 individuals from various departments in his company to talk about anything. On a weekly basis, he and his supervisors would have lunch with the upper management of his largest supplier, the Kodak Apparatus Division, which provided one-third of the components utilized in the design and production processes. In a later version he coined "business meetings," twelve to twenty personnel are brought together by their bosses to discuss a predetermined subject, like master scheduling or inventory. The objective is to ensure that every one of his 1,500 employees attends one of these annual business meetings.

Writing was another tool that Trowbridge and Crandall used to further their cause. Monthly, staff members would receive a *Copy Products Journal* that ranged in length from four to eight pages. Workers were able to pose queries to Crandall and his upper management in an anonymous setting through a programme known as "Dialogue Letters" and were assured of a response. However, the charts were the most prominent and impactful written information. These massive charts, displayed in a main hallway next to the cafeteria, showed the outcomes of each product's quality, pricing and delivery according to challenging benchmarks. Distributed across the production area were one hundred miniature reproductions of these charts, each detailing the expenses and quality standards of a different work group.

It took six months for the first signs of success from this rigorous alignment process to emerge, and another year brought even more clarity. Thanks to these victories, the message gained credibility and more people joined the cause. One of the primary product lines saw a quality boost of over 100 times between 1984 and 1988. The defect rate decreased from 30 to 0.3 per unit. Costs for a different product line decreased by roughly 24 per cent over a three-year period. From 1985 to 1987, there was an increase from 82 per cent to 95 per cent of on-time deliveries. Despite a rise in product volume, inventory levels fell by more than 50 per cent from 1984 to 1988. Additionally, output per manufacturing worker increased by a factor of two between 1985 and 1988.

Management builds its ability to carry out its plan through organizing and staffing. This entails making a set of jobs and an organizational structure to meet the plan's requirements, filling those jobs with competent people, informing those people of the plan, giving them responsibility for carrying it out and then coming up with ways to monitor how well it's being implemented. Aligning individuals, on the other hand, is the same as leadership. To do this, the new course of action must be communicated to individuals with the ability to form coalitions whose members share the vision and are dedicated to seeing it through.

In the end, management makes sure the plan gets done by managing and fixing problems. This includes keeping an eye on how well actual results match up with the plan, both formally and informally through reports, meetings and other tools. If there are any deviations, management plans and organizes to fix them. Achieving a vision, however, is the job of leaders who can inspire and motivate their followers to keep going in the face of enormous resistance to change by speaking to their most fundamental and frequently unexplored values, emotions and wants.

The abilities required of leaders can be better understood by taking a deeper look at each of these tasks.

Choosing a Path vs Preparing and Allocating Funds

Leadership boils down to determining the course of action for bringing about change, since that is the very essence of leadership. Although the two are frequently confused, setting direction is not the same as planning, even long-term planning. Management planning is logical in nature and aims to bring about orderly outcomes rather than change. Offering guidance is more of an inductive process. A leader's job is to sift through mountains of data in search of connections, patterns and explanations. Also, leadership isn't just about making plans; it's also about making vision and strategy. Such documents lay out the ideal future state of a company, product or company culture and provide a path towards that state.

When people talk about visions, it usually turns into something mystical. The idea is that having a vision is something esoteric that no one, no matter how gifted, could ever achieve. However, there is no secret formula for creating sound company strategy. Data collection and analysis is a challenging and, at times, draining process. Those who can express such dreams aren't sorcerers, but rather risk-takers with a broad strategic mind.

Neither do goals and plans need to be wildly original; in fact, many great ones aren't. Successful company goals often include concepts that are already widely recognized and have a quite ordinary nature. The concepts themselves may not be novel, but their specific arrangement or patterning might be.

If we take Scandinavian Airlines System (SAS) as an example, when CEO Jan Carlzon stated his goal of making SAS the premier airline for business travellers, it was common knowledge among those working in the field. Compared to other market categories, business travellers fly more frequently and are typically willing to pay higher tickets. So, if an airline targets business travellers, it may see consistent revenue, large profit margins and rapid expansion. However, no business in an industry notorious for red tape has ever committed to putting these basic concepts into action. As a result, SAS was successful.

A vision's uniqueness is less significant than how effectively it satisfies the interests of key constituents, including as consumers, investors and employees, and how quickly it can be transformed into a practical competitive strategy. To put it another way, bad visions often put the interests of key constituencies—like employees—above those of customers or stockholders. They may also be poorly planned. Talk of reaching number one in an industry by a company that has never been better than a weak opponent is the stuff of pipe dreams, not visions.

Companies that are overly managed and underled often make the mistake of thinking that long-term planning will solve all of their problems, including being unable to respond to changes in the market and staying ahead of the competition. However, this strategy is flawed since it fails to take into account the fundamentals of defining goals.

It takes time to plan for the future. Every time something out of the ordinary occurs, plans need to be rethought. Planning for the future may become an extremely tedious task in a fast-paced corporate world where surprises are commonplace. That is why the best companies keep their planning processes so short-lived. In fact, there are many who see "long-term planning" as an oxymoron.

In 1979, when Lou Gerstner took over as president of American Express's Travel Related Services (TRS) division, the division was confronting one of the most significant difficulties it had ever faced in its 130-year existence. In an effort to undercut American Express, hundreds of financial institutions are either already selling or are in the process of launching Visa and MasterCard credit cards. Additionally, over twenty other financial institutions were entering the traveller's check market. Margin reduction and growth prohibition are common outcomes of increased competition in established markets.

However, Gerstner had a different vision for the company. His five years of consulting for TRS, where he oversaw the travel division's money-losing operations and the card operation's growing competitiveness, prepared him for his role as an analyst for American Express. Gerstner and his group drilled down into the company's inner workings by asking crucial questions on the market, competitors and economics. While doing so, he started to create an image of TRS that was at odds with the reality of a 130-year-old firm operating in an established market.

Even though thousands of banks were vying for customers with Visa and MasterCard, Gerstner believed TRS could become a dynamic and expanding industry. The trick was to zero in on the international market and, more especially, on the relatively well-off clientele that American Express had long catered to with its premium offerings. Customers with more disposable income could purchase more services from TRS than before because the company aggressively developed a wide range of new products and services, invested to increase productivity and decrease costs, and further segmented the market.

Gerstner convened the card organization's top brass within a week of taking office and cast doubt on every guiding concept by which they operated. It was two things that he questioned that others generally agreed upon: first, that the division should only sell the green card, and second, that the product had little room for improvement.

Additionally, Gerstner wasted no time in establishing a more entrepreneurial culture, recruiting and educating individuals who would flourish in it and communicating the big picture to them. Smart risk-taking was rewarded by him and other upper-level managers. Unnecessary bureaucracy was discouraged in order to facilitate entrepreneurship. Additionally, they instituted more stringent hiring procedures and established the TRS Graduate Management Programme to provide exceptional training, a richer array of opportunities, and an unprecedented level of interaction with senior management to young individuals with great promise. Gerstner also instituted a programme to acknowledge and reward outstanding customer service—a key component of TRS's vision—in an effort to promote risk-taking among all workers.

The emergence of new markets, products and services was spurred on by these incentives. TRS significantly increased its global footprint. There were 29 different currencies that American Express cards could be used in by 1988, up from 11 a decade earlier. In addition, the unit made a concerted effort to target women and college students, two demographics that had previously been underserved. To better assist its corporate customers in keeping tabs on their travel budgets, TRS integrated its card and travel-service offerings in 1981. Furthermore, AmEx had expanded to the point where it was the fifth biggest direct mail retailer in the US by 1988.

Also introduced were a Platinum American Express card, Optima, a revolving credit card, and 90 days of purchase protection with every AmEx purchase. A more user-friendly monthly statement and a 25 per cent drop in billing expenses resulted from the company's 1988 use of image-processing technology for billing.

The net income of TRS soared by an astounding 500 per cent between 1978 and 1987, a compounded yearly rate of around 18 per cent, all because of these advances. A lot of so-called high-tech, high-growth enterprises couldn't match the company's performance. Its return on equity in 1988 was 28 per cent, which was higher than the average for low-growth, high-profit companies.

When a business lacks focus, even near-term strategies have the potential to spiral out of control and consume all available resources. If there is no overarching goal or strategy to direct or limit the planning process, then every possible outcome should have a strategy. In such a situation, backup plans might drag on indefinitely, taking resources away from more pressing matters, all the while failing to offer the much-needed clarity of purpose that a business requires. The planning process has the potential to become an extremely politicized game when managers eventually get jaded.

Rather than replacing it, planning is most effective when used in conjunction with direction setting. An effective planning approach can help keep direction-setting activities grounded in reality. Similarly, planning can be carried out realistically when a competent direction-setting procedure has provided a focus. This aids in distinguishing between necessary and superfluous planning.

Shifting Focus from Organizing and Staffing to Aligning People

Employees in today's organizations are interdependent on one another through their job, technology, management systems and organizational hierarchy; as a result, no one has full autonomy. When organizations strive to transform, these connections pose a unique obstacle. People have a tendency to tumble over one other until a large number of people join forces and go in the same direction. Getting everyone pulling in the same direction seems like an organizational problem to CEOs who have a management degree but no leadership training. However, CEOs should focus on aligning rather than organizing their teams.

When managers 'organize' their teams, they make it possible for them to carry out plans with pinpoint accuracy and maximum efficiency. In most cases, this calls for a slew of choices, some of which could be tricky. The following are some of the many tasks that an organization must complete: establish a reporting structure, hire qualified people for each position, train employees as needed, share goals and objectives with employees, and decide how much power to provide to each employee. In addition to tools to track the plan's execution, financial incentives should be put in place to make it a reality. Comparable to architectural considerations are these organizational evaluations. It all comes down to how well it fits in with the given situation.

Contrast with alignment. The issue is less with the design and more with the communication surrounding it. When compared to organizing, aligning always requires more one-on-one communication. Not only can a manager's subordinates be part of the target population, but so can their supervisors, colleagues, employees from other departments, vendors, regulators and consumers. Relevant individuals include those who can either aid in or obstruct the execution of the vision and tactics.

It seems like there's an organizational issue with the idea of encouraging individuals to move in the same direction. However, CEOs should focus on aligning rather than organizing their teams.

There is a vast difference in the communications problem of organizing people to complete a short-term goal and the task of trying to convince them to understand a vision of an alternative future. It's like a football quarterback having to convey to his squad a brand new strategy for the second half of the season versus trying to discuss the next two or three plays.

The mere fact that a message is comprehended does not guarantee its acceptance, regardless of how many words or symbols are used to convey it. Credibility, or persuading others to believe the message, is another major obstacle for leadership initiatives. Factors that add weight to a message's credibility include the speaker's reputation for honesty and reliability, the message's substance, the speaker's past performance and the congruence between the speaker's words and actions.

Lastly, unlike organizing, aligning actually empowers people. For some businesses, the widespread sense of helplessness is a major factor in their inability to respond quickly enough to shifts in consumer demand and technological capabilities. Experience has taught them that even if they accurately identify significant external developments and take the necessary steps to address them, they are still susceptible to criticism from higher-ups. Disciplinary actions can be expressed in a variety of ways: "That's against policy," "We can't afford it" or simply "Shut up and do as I say."

People are empowered in at least two ways through alignment, which helps to solve this challenge. Secondly, when the organization-wide vision has been conveyed, lower-level staff are able to take the lead without feeling as exposed. Their supervisors will have an easier time reprimanding them if their actions align with the vision. Second, with everyone pulling in the same direction, there's less chance that one person's plan will get derailed because it clashes with another's.

Inspiring Others Rather Than Dominating Them and Resolving Their Issues

Being ability to produce highly energized behaviour is critical for overcoming the unavoidable obstacles to change, since change is a leadership role. Successful motivation guarantees that individuals will have the energy to overcome barriers, similar to how direction setting indicates a suitable path for movement and good alignment gets people moving down that road.

Management theory states that control mechanisms should monitor system performance against the plan and respond appropriately to any discrepancies. For instance, in an efficiently run factory, this would entail that the planning phase sets reasonable quality goals, the organizing phase creates a structure capable of reaching those goals, and the control phase ensures that quality breaches are detected and rectified without delay (rather than after 30 or 60 days).

Management relies heavily on control, which is why intrinsically driven or inspired actions are largely unimportant. There can be no room for error or risk in a manager's procedures. This precludes their reliance on anything out of the ordinary or difficult to procure. Systematic approaches exist to facilitate the day-to-day accomplishment of mundane tasks by ordinarily behaving individuals. It lacks glitz and glamour. That, however, is management.

9

Go, Get It: The CEO Who Motivates

Over the course of almost twenty years following its establishment in 1956, the paper products subsidiary of Procter & Gamble had seen very little competition for its consumer goods that were of high quality, competitively priced and exceptionally effectively promoted. Nevertheless, by the late 1970s, the division's position in the market had gone through a transformation. New competitive thrusts are terrible for Procter & Gamble. Taking disposable diapers as an example, analysts in the industry estimate that the company's market share for these products dropped from 75 per cent in the middle of the 1970s to 52 per cent in 1984.

After spending three years working in the more compact and rapidly expanding soft drink business for Procter & Gamble, Richard Nicolosi made the transition to paper goods in that year as the associate general manager. Upon his arrival, he discovered a very bureaucratic and centralized organization that was excessively focused on the accomplishment of internal technical objectives and projects. The vast majority of the information regarding customers was obtained through in-depth quantitative market research. Both the commercial people and the technical people were almost at war with each other. The commercial people concentrated on volume and share, while the technical people were paid for how much money they saved.

In the latter part of the summer of 1984, the upper management made the announcement that Nicolosi would be promoted to the position of head of paper goods in October. By August of that same year, he had already begun to informally supervise the division. Right on, he started emphasizing how important it was for the division to expand its creative capabilities and become more market-oriented, rather than merely focusing on becoming a low-cost producer. After some time had passed, Nicolosi claimed that he had to make it abundantly obvious that the rules of the game had been altered.

A considerably larger emphasis was placed on teamwork and multiple leadership roles as part of the new direction. Nicolosi advocated for the utilization of groups as a management approach for the division and the items that it specialized in. In the month of October, he and his staff decided to establish themselves as the 'board' of the paper division and started meeting on a monthly basis, and later on a weekly basis. In November, they began delegating authority to the "category teams" that they had developed in order to handle their big brand groups, which included things like diapers, tissues and towels. Nicolosi emphasized that one should "go for the leap" rather than "seek the incremental."

Throughout the month of December, Nicolosi participated in a number of activities in a more selected and detailed manner. During his meeting with the advertising agency, he became acquainted with key creative individuals. Additionally, he requested that the marketing manager of diapers report directly to him, which would remove one level from the organizational hierarchy. More of his conversations were with those individuals who were engaged in the process of developing new products.

An announcement on a new organizational structure was made by the board in January of 1985. This new structure featured not only category teams but also new-brand business teams. By the time spring arrived, the board was prepared to organize a significant motivating event with the goal of conveying the vision for the new paper goods to the greatest number of people possible. The local Masonic Temple was the location where a gathering of several thousand individuals took place on 4 June 1985. Everyone who worked in the paper industry in Cincinnati, including sales district managers and paper plant managers, was present. Nicolosi and the other members of the board shared their vision of an organization in which "each of us is a leader for the organization." The event was captured on camera, and a version that had been edited was distributed to all of the facilities and sales offices so that everyone could watch it.

All of these actions contributed to the establishment of an entrepreneurial climate, which, in turn, inspired a significant number of individuals to bring the new vision into reality. People who worked with new items were the source of the majority of inventions. The introduction of Ultra Pampers in February 1985 resulted in an increase in the market share of the total Pampers product line from 40 per cent to 58 per cent, as well as an increase in profitability from zero to positive. Over the course of just a few short months, the market share of the Luvs Delux brand increased by a factor of 150 per cent after it was first introduced in May of 1987.

Other initiatives taken by employees were more focused on a particular functional area, and some of them originated from the lowest levels of the organizational hierarchy. After experiencing a sense of empowerment as a result of the new culture, a few of the division's secretaries decided to establish a secretarial network in the spring of 1986. Training, awards and recognition, and the "secretary of the future" are the topics that were discussed in the subcommittees that were constituted by this association.

The thoughts of many of her colleagues were echoed by one of the paper products secretaries, who stated, "I don't see why we, too, can't contribute to the division's new direction."

Over a span of four years, the paper products division's revenues had increased by 40 per cent by the time 1988 came to a close. The profits increased by 68 per cent. Moreover, this transpired in spite of the fact that the level of competition continued to increase.

It is not the same as leadership. There is always a need for a surge of energy in order to accomplish lofty ideas. People are energized by motivation and inspiration, not because control systems drive them in the right way, but rather because they meet fundamental human wants such as the need for achievement, a sense of belonging, recognition, self-esteem, a sense of control over one's life and the opportunity to live up to one's ideals. Feelings like these have a profound impact on us and provoke a strong reaction from us.

Motivation can be achieved in a variety of ways by effective leaders. To begin, they guarantee that the vision of the organization is always articulated in a manner that places an emphasis on the values of the audience that they are speaking to. Because of this, the effort is significant to the folks in question. In addition, leaders frequently involve members of the staff in the process of determining how to realize the organization's vision (or the aspect of the vision that is most pertinent to a certain individual). People will feel more in control as a result of this. In addition to being an important method of motivation, it is also necessary to support the efforts of employees to realize the vision by offering coaching, feedback and role modelling. This helps people improve professionally and enhances their self-esteem. The last point is that effective leaders acknowledge and reward success, which not only provides individuals with a feeling of accomplishment but also gives them the impression that they are a part of an organization that is concerned about them. Following the completion of all of these tasks, the work itself will become intrinsically engaging.

Leaders have a greater responsibility to inspire their followers to take on leadership roles in proportion to the degree to which the corporate environment is characterized by change. In situations when this strategy is successful, it has the potential to replicate leadership throughout the entire organization, with individuals occupying several leadership roles at various levels of command. The fact that a large number of individuals are need to take initiative in order to successfully manage change in any complicated firm makes this extremely valuable. Any less than that will not do.

Without a doubt, leadership that originates from a variety of sources does not necessarily coexist. Contrarily, it is prone to conflicting with other things. To ensure that people are able to work together effectively in numerous leadership roles, it is necessary to carefully coordinate the actions of individuals using processes that are distinct from those used to coordinate traditional management responsibilities.

People are energized not by being pushed in the proper path, but rather by having their fundamental human needs satisfied. This is how motivation and inspiration work.

The coordination of leadership activities is facilitated by robust networks of informal relationships, which are the kind of interactions that may be found in businesses that have healthy cultures. This is similar to the way that formal structure is used to coordinate management tasks. The most important distinction is that informal networks are able to deal with the increased needs for coordination that are associated with activities that are not routine and when there is change. The numerous communication channels and the trust that exists between the individuals who are connected through those channels make it possible for a continual process of accommodating and adapting to new circumstances. When there are disagreements between positions, the same relationships that help resolve the disagreements are also helpful. This process of conversation and adaptation can develop visions that are linked and compatible rather than distant and competitive. This is perhaps the most important and significant aspect of the process. In contrast to formal structures, strong informal networks are able to handle the amount of communication that is required to coordinate administrative functions. All of this demands a significant deal more communication than is required.

The existence of informal relations of some kind can be found in any corporation. But all too frequently, these networks are either extremely weak—some individuals are well linked, but the majority of them are not—or they are highly fragmented—a strong network exists within the marketing group and within R&D, but it does not exist between the two departments. These kinds of networks are not very effective in supporting numerous leadership agendas. In point of fact, extensive informal networks are of such significance that, in the event that they do not already exist, its creation must be the primary focus of effort at the beginning of a significant leadership initiative.

A Culture of Leadership That Is Being Created

In spite of the fact that leadership is becoming an increasingly important factor in the success of businesses, the majority of people's experiences on the job appear to be detrimental to the development of the qualities that are necessary for leadership careers. Nevertheless, there are some businesses that have continuously shown that they are capable of elevating individuals to the level of exceptional leaders and managers. Recruiting individuals who have the potential to take on leadership roles is just the first step. Managing their career habits is also an important aspect to consider. In many cases, individuals who are successful in significant leadership jobs have a variety of career experiences in common with one another.

One of the most common and significant challenges that one encounters early on in their profession is the substantial challenge. It is nearly always the case that leaders have had opportunities during their twenties and thirties to genuinely try to lead, to take risks and to learn from both their successes and their mistakes. It would appear that this kind of learning is necessary in order to cultivate a diverse set of leadership abilities and thoughts. In addition, people learn something about the challenges of leadership as well as the potential for it to bring about change through the chances that are presented to them.

Later on in their careers, they experience something that is equally significant and has to do with widening their horizons. It is always possible for individuals who give good leadership in significant occupations to have the opportunity to grow beyond the narrow basis that is characteristic of the majority of managerial careers before they even begin working in such jobs. The majority of the time, this occurs as a consequence of lateral career movements or early promotions to exceptionally extensive occupational responsibilities. In some cases, additional resources, such as specialized task-force assignments or an extensive general management course, can be of use. No matter what the circumstances are, the breadth of information that can be acquired through this method appears to be beneficial in all facets of leadership. This is also true for the network of contacts that are frequently cultivated both within and beyond the confines of the organization. Whenever a sufficient number of individuals are provided with opportunities such as these, the relationships that are formed also contribute to the formation of robust informal networks that are required to sustain various leadership projects.

People who are able to successfully produce leaders are typically recognized and rewarded by businesses that are well-led.

Companies that perform a better-than-average job of training leaders in their workforce place a strong emphasis on providing relatively young employees with opportunities to overcome hard situations. Decentralization is the key to success in many areas of business. By definition, it is a method of distributing responsibility farther downward within an organization, which in turn results in the creation of positions that are more difficult at lower levels. Companies like as Johnson & Johnson, 3M, Hewlett-Packard and General Electric, along with a great number of other well-known businesses, have utilized that strategy with great success. As a result of the fact that some of those same corporations also build as many little units as they possibly can, there are a great deal of tough tasks available in general management at lower levels.

There are times when these companies create additional opportunities that are tough by putting an emphasis on growth through the introduction of new products or services. One of the policies that 3M has adhered to over the years is that at least 25 per cent of its income should originate from items that have been released within the past five years. This fosters the formation of new, smaller businesses, which, in turn, provide hundreds of opportunities for young people who have the potential to become leaders to be tested and stretched.

These types of activities have the potential to nearly entirely train individuals for leadership positions in small and medium-sized businesses. But senior executives need to put in more effort, and it typically takes a considerable amount of time, in order to cultivate individuals who are capable of holding major leadership roles. The first step in this task is to make an effort to identify individuals who have the potential to become great leaders at an early stage in their careers and to determine what will be required to stretch and develop those individuals.

Once more, this procedure does not have any sort of wizardry to it. In a surprising way, the strategies that successful businesses employ are rather easy. Within their organizations, they go to great lengths to ensure that younger workers and those working at lower levels are brought to the attention of top management staff. After that, senior managers make their own determinations regarding who possesses potential and what the requirements for development are for those individuals. Executives also engage in a discussion among themselves over their provisional conclusions in order to arrive at more precise judgements.

Executives in these firms then spend time preparing for the growth of their employees now that they have a clear understanding of who among their employees have significant leadership potential and what skills they need to improve. As part of a formal succession planning or high-potential development process, this may be done on occasion; nevertheless, the majority of the time, it is done in a more casual manner. In either scenario, it seems that the most important component is an educated evaluation of what kinds of growth chances are achievable and meet the requirements of each individual candidate.

Many firms that are led effectively have a tendency to recognize and reward individuals who successfully create leaders. This is done in order to encourage managers to participate in these activities. For the very reason that it is so difficult to assess such accomplishments with precision, this is something that is rarely done as part of a formal compensation or bonus calculation. However, it does become a consideration in the judgements that are made regarding promotions, particularly to the highest levels of seniority, and this appears to make a significant difference. Even individuals who maintain that leadership is not something that can be cultivated in any way discover ways to develop it when they are informed that their future promotions would depend, at least in part, on their capacity to cultivate prospective leaders.

These tactics contribute to the establishment of a company culture in which individuals place a high value on great leadership and work to develop it. In the same way that we require more individuals to take on leadership roles in the intricate organizations that are the norm in our society today, we also require more individuals to cultivate the cultures that will be responsible for producing leadership. What constitutes the pinnacle of leadership is the establishment of a culture that is centred on leadership.

10

See Inside, CEO: Finding Your Authentic Self

Over the last half-century, researchers in the field of leadership have poured over a thousand studies into the question of what makes a successful leader. So far, no study has been able to pin down the perfect leader. I am grateful. People would be constantly attempting to mimic a leadership style that academics had created if it were a set formula. They would transform into characters instead of real individuals, and everyone would be able to tell.

If you want to be genuine, you can't try to be someone else. While it's true that you can gain wisdom from the mistakes of others, striving to mimic their achievement will lead you nowhere. When you show up as yourself and not a carbon copy of someone else, people will trust you more. After gaining invaluable experience as Jack Welch's assistant in the 1980s, Amgen CEO and president Kevin Sharer observed the dark side of GE's cult of personality. "Becoming like Jack was the goal of everyone," he says. Leadership is a multi-faceted concept. Stop trying to be someone else and just be yourself.

A severe lack of faith in authoritative figures has grown among the populace in recent years. A different type of corporate leader is clearly required in the modern era. *Authentic Leadership:*

Rediscovering the Secrets to Creating Lasting Value, written by Bill George in 2003, issued a challenge to a new generation to lead with authenticity. Genuine leaders are enthusiastic about what they do, always act in accordance with their principles and guide their teams with both logic and emotion. They are able to self-discipline themselves to achieve their goals and build relationships that endure. They are self-assured.

Since this was a pressing issue, our study group decided to investigate the following: "How can people become and remain authentic leaders?" For this study, we surveyed 125 leaders to find out what made a difference in their leadership development. This interview-based research of leadership development is the most extensive of its kind. The people we spoke with were quite forthcoming about their life experiences, including the ups and downs, challenges and moments of success or failure that led them to realize their full potential.

A dedication to personal growth is necessary to uncover your own leadership potential. You have to commit yourself for the rest of your life to reaching your full potential, just like athletes and musicians do. According to Kroger CEO David Dillon, the majority of successful leaders he has worked with were self-taught. If you want a growth plan from your employer, you can't expect to get one handed to you, according to Dillon. Taking charge of your own growth is something you must do.

Reflecting on Your Life's Journey

Gaining insight into your life's narrative is the first step towards being a genuine leader. An individual's life narrative gives meaning to their experiences and can serve as a source of motivation for making a difference in the world. "Your life's narrative is not your life," said author John Barth. What counts most, not the cold, hard facts of your life, is the tale you choose to tell about it. The story of your life is like a tape that never ends playing in your mind. In your quest to understand who you are and where you fit in the world, you may find yourself replaying significant life events and encounters.

While genuine leaders' narratives encompass a wide range of influences, including those of parents, coaches, instructors and mentors, many have said that a traumatic event served as a turning point in their lives. Their stories revealed the profound impact of a number of life-altering events, including unemployment, serious sickness, the sudden passing of a loved one, social exclusion, prejudice and rejection. But genuine leaders didn't perceive themselves as victims; they found purpose in these defining moments. In reinterpreting these occurrences, they were able to overcome their obstacles and find their calling as leaders.

Embracing Your True Identity

Self-awareness is the most crucial quality for leaders to cultivate. But many leaders, particularly those just starting out, are so focused on making a name for themselves that they neglect to take the time to learn about themselves. Money, celebrity, power, position or an increase in stock price are some of the externally recognized metrics that they aim to achieve. They may achieve temporary professional success thanks to their ambition, but they often fail to maintain that level of achievement. They may come to realize they aren't living up to their full potential as they become older and realize something is missing from their lives. In order to get to know one's true self, one must be brave enough to go within and honestly evaluate one's past. Doing so makes leaders more empathetic and open to showing their vulnerabilities.

Nearly all 75 members of the Advisory Council at Stanford

University's Graduate School of Business agreed that self-awareness is the most crucial quality for leaders to cultivate. David Pottruck, the former CEO of Charles Schwab, had a particularly tenacious path to self-awareness among the executives we spoke with. Pottruck was named the University of Pennsylvania's Most Valuable Player after being a high school football all-leaguer. He worked for Citigroup after earning his MBA from Wharton and then relocated to San Francisco to become the head of marketing for Charles Schwab. Pottruck, who was a tremendous worker, failed to grasp why his new coworkers disliked his relentless pursuit of goals and the many hours he put in. After all, he had hoped that his achievements would be sufficient evidence. "Because I was focused on contributing to the company's success, the idea that my high energy levels could be intimidating or offensive to others never crossed my mind."

As Pottruck reflected, "That feedback was like a dagger to my heart." The news that his coworkers did not trust him startled him. Since I disagreed with how other people perceived me, I remained in a state of denial. I was unaware of how selfish I came across to others until I became a source of tension. Still, deep down I knew the criticism was accurate. Pottruck understood he couldn't achieve unless he conquered his blind spots.

When it comes to developing self-awareness, leaders may find that denial is the biggest obstacle.

When it comes to developing self-awareness, leaders may find that denial is the biggest obstacle. Each of them has pride that needs stroking, doubts that need easing and fears that need calming. Genuine leaders know they need to be receptive to criticism, even when it's negative. "After my second marriage fell apart, I thought I had a wife-selection problem." Then, he worked with a counsellor who delivered some hard truths: "The good news is you do not have a wife-selection problem; the bad news is you have a husband-behaviour problem." Pottruck then made a determined effort to change after finally realising he still had large blind spots. I felt like a man who has had three heart attacks and has finally come to the realization that he needs to stop smoking and reduce weight, as he put it.

These days, Pottruck is content in his new marriage and pays close attention when his wife gives him helpful criticism. Even though he has learned to manage stress better, he still occasionally reverts to his old methods, especially when he's under a lot of pressure. I am able to accept criticism without denying it because I have achieved enough achievement in life to have sufficient self-respect. Rather of beating myself up over little setbacks, I have finally figured out how to deal with disappointment and failure.

Living According to Your Principles and Values

Your convictions and beliefs are the wellspring of the values that underpin genuine leadership, but you can't tell what your values really are until you put them to the test. When you're on top of the world, it's easy to write down your ideals and stick to them. You discover your priorities, your level of sacrifice and your ability to make trade-offs when your success, career or even life is on the line.

Leadership principles are the ideals that make up a leader's code of conduct. If you want to be a good leader, you need to have strong ideals that you can put to the test. "Create a work environment where people are respected for their contributions, provided job security and allowed to fulfil their potential" might be a leadership concept that translates a value like "concern for others" into action.

Think about Jon Huntsman, who started Huntsman Corporation and is now its chairman. Working for Nixon in 1972, just before Watergate, severely tested his moral principles. After a brief stint in the U.S. while working for the HEW department, he was employed by H.R. Haldeman, the influential chief of staff of President Nixon. According to Huntsman, following Haldeman's directives was a "very mixed" experience. They had some disagreements because Haldeman wanted to undertake a lot of dubious things, and I wasn't prepared to follow orders regardless of their moral or ethical validity. There was an immoral vibe all over the White House.

Haldeman once told Huntsman to help him capture a congressman from California who was fighting against a White House programme. It had been revealed that the lawmaker was a co-owner of a plant that hired individuals without proper documentation. In an undercover operation at the congressman's plant, Haldeman instructed Huntsman to have the plant manager of a company that Huntsman owned place several undocumented workers in order to obtain information that would humiliate the congressman.

"There are moments when we respond hastily and don't always discern between right and wrong," Huntsman reflected. "For some reason, I didn't give this much consideration. Although my gut told me it was wrong, the realization didn't sink in for a while. In the fifteen minutes that followed, my conscience finally spoke out and told me this wasn't a good choice. My core values, which had been with me from the beginning, were active. I told our plant manager, 'Let's not do this,' midway through our meeting. 'That game isn't something I'm interested in playing. In case you forgot, I called.'

"This was not how Huntsman would use his people, he assured Haldeman. I was politely declining an offer from the country's number two executive. Such replies, which he perceived as indications of betrayal, were not appreciated by him. I should have just said goodbye. Well, then. It was less than six months before I departed."

Keeping Your Intrinsic and Extrinsic Drives in Check

Understanding what motivates you is essential for true leaders because it helps them maintain balance in their life and high levels of motivation. Intrinsic and extrinsic motives are the two main categories. Despite their reluctance to acknowledge it, many leaders are driven to succeed by constantly comparing themselves to external standards. They take pleasure in the acclaim and social standing that accompany promotions and salary increases. Conversely, people's sense of life's purpose is the source of their intrinsic motivations. They are intricately related to the narrative of one's life and how it is portrayed. Personal development, assisting others in their development, tackling social issues and creating a positive impact on the world are all examples. The trick is to satisfy both your need for approval from others and the internal drives that make your job worthwhile.

Several interviewees cautioned budding leaders against succumbing to societal, peer or parental pressures. A longtime executive at Hewlett-Packard in Silicon Valley, Debra Dunn, said, "The path of accumulating material possessions is clearly laid out," referring to the persistent demands from outside forces. Counting it is something you're familiar with. The world will look at you strangely if you don't go down that road. Knowing what makes you happy and fulfilled is the first step in staying away from materialism.

Giving up the need for other people to approve of your success isn't always a walk in the park. It requires guts to follow one's own fundamental motives once an achievement-oriented leader becomes accustomed to a string of successes throughout their formative years. However, in order to achieve lasting success, most leaders eventually realize they must tackle more challenging issues. Alice Woodwark, a 29-year-old with a successful career at McKinsey, reflected on her own naive conception of performance, which stemmed from lessons she acquired about validation and praise as a child. However, there is little use in rushing towards something significant if all you're doing is following after the rabbit as it runs around the course.

When compared to extrinsic motivations, intrinsic ones are more satisfying and in line with your values.

Putting Up Your Backbone

Leaders require others to help them succeed; not even the most self-assured CEOs can do it alone. You might easily become lost if you don't have solid relationships to keep you grounded.

True leaders, in order to keep themselves afloat, assemble remarkable support systems. They receive guidance from those groups when they are unsure of what to do, assistance when things go tough and shared joy when things are good. Whenever leaders are going through tough times, they find solace in being around supportive individuals who they can confide in and let their guard down. Friends that accept them for who they are, flaws and all, are treasured during their lowest moments. Genuine leaders discover that the people they surround themselves with offer them validation, wisdom, new perspectives and, when necessary, a nudge in the right direction.

In order to establish a support system, what steps must one take? In addition to their families, friends, mentors and coworkers, most genuine leaders also rely on their spouses or significant others. They gradually expand their networks as the trust and confidence they need during times of difficulty and uncertainty are built via shared experiences, histories and openness with those closest to them. For leaders to build connections that are mutually beneficial, they must give to their followers just as much as they receive from them.

It all begins with finding someone who accepts you no matter what—flaws and all—and who you are as a whole. Truthfully, that somebody is often the only one you can trust to tell you the whole truth. Although some leaders form these ties with other members of their family, friends or a trusted mentor, most leaders find that their spouse is the one with whom they have the deepest relationships. Being able to depend on unwavering support increases the likelihood that leaders will accept themselves authentically.

The final indicator of a genuine leader is exceptional performance maintained over an extended length of time.

When people show they care about one other and want to accomplish the same things, many relationships flourish. His marriage to Debra Dunn, an employee at Hewlett-Packard, is lasting, according to Randy Komisar of the venture capital firm Kleiner Perkins Caufield & Byers, since their beliefs are similar. "Our individual goals, principles, and values are quite congruent, yet Debra and I are highly autonomous. Questions like 'What will you leave behind in this world?' reverberate deeply with us. Our life goals should be in harmony with one another."

A life-altering mentor has touched the lives of many leaders. Mentoring relationships that work best encourage both parties to learn from one another, discover areas of common ground and have fun together. A mentor-mentee relationship will not endure if the mentee is solely interested in the mentor's professional success and not in the mentor's personal life. What keeps the link going is the fact that it is mutually beneficial.

Numerous kinds exist for both personal and professional support networks. One of the Piper Jaffray characters, Tad Piper, is an AA member. They are not chief executive officers, he said. In their efforts to remain sober, live decent lives and support one another in being vulnerable, honest and open, they are simply a collection of wonderful, hardworking individuals. As we progress through the 12 stages, we support one other's actions by having disciplined conversations about our chemical dependency. Being in the company of folks who aren't merely talking about these kinds of issues but are actively working to address them makes me feel fortunate.

Similar to Piper, Bill George joined a men's group in 1974 following a weekend retreat. Every Wednesday morning, the group continues to meet, even after more than 30 years. One of the eight people in the group takes the lead in discussing a subject he has chosen after an introductory session of catching up and addressing any specific challenges anybody may be experiencing. These conversations are free-flowing, in-depth and frequently insightful. People are able to speak their minds without worrying about what others will think of them, which is a major factor in their success. Because it provides a safe space to share and receive constructive criticism when needed and helps members to better understand and articulate their core values and principles, the group is highly valued by all members.

Making Your Life Fit by Maintaining a Firm Foundation

One of the biggest obstacles leaders encounter is integrating their lives. To live a well-rounded life, you must unite all of its parts—your job, your family, your community and your friends—so that you may remain authentic no matter where you are. Imagine your life as a house divided into different rooms: the bedroom for your private life, the study for your work life, the family room for your loved ones and the living room for socialising with friends. Could you possibly be the same person in all of these rooms if you tore down the barriers between them?

Consider your life as a dwelling. Would it be possible to be one person in multiple rooms if you tore down the walls between them?

True authenticity, according to John Donahoe (ex-worldwide managing director of Bain and current president of eBay Marketplaces), entails being true to oneself no matter the circumstances. "If you allow it, the world can shape you," he said. Making deliberate decisions allows you to maintain a feeling of identity throughout your life. There are moments when you have to make tough decisions and mess up frequently.

An assured and steady demeanour is a hallmark of genuine leadership. People don't perceive them as changing personas day to day. It takes self-control to integrate, especially when things get tough and you want to respond badly or revert to old behaviours. Donahoe is certain that he has grown into a better leader as a result of integrating his life. "Nirvana does not exist," he declares. The trade-offs don't get any easier as you get older, so the fight is continual. However, genuine leaders know that their personal and professional life aren't competing objectives. I can say with absolute certainty that having children has transformed me into a far more capable leader at work, as Donahoe put it. It all came down to having a solid personal life.

Leading is a demanding occupation. Managing people, organizations, outcomes and the ever-changing environmental variables is an incredibly stressful job. The farther you climb, the more influence you have over your own fate, but you'll also be under more stress. Instead of asking if stress is avoidable, you should ask how to manage it so that you can keep your own equilibrium.

Truthful leaders know how critical it is to have a steady footing. Aside from spending time with loved ones, genuine leaders also make time to exercise, practise spirituality, serve their communities and visit their hometowns. They are able to remain genuine leaders because of all of these things.

Helping Individuals Take the Lead

Since we've covered how to find your true leadership style, let's examine how genuine leaders—the ultimate goal of any leader—enable their teams to accomplish remarkable things in the long run.

True leaders know that being a leader isn't about achieving personal achievement or amassing a devoted following of followers. They are cognizant of the fact that empowered leaders—including those without direct reports—are essential to any thriving organization. In addition to being an inspiration, they give others around them the confidence to take the lead.

Chairman and CEO Anne Mulcahy's remarkable turnaround of Xerox was greatly influenced by her reputation for establishing strong relationships and empowering individuals. At the time that Xerox invited Mulcahy to succeed her unsuccessful predecessor, the corporation was $18 billion in debt and had used up all of its available credit. Employee morale plummeted as the stock price plummeted. The situation was exacerbated since the company's revenue recognition processes were under investigation by the SEC.

No one, not even Mulcahy herself, was expecting her appointment. She was a 25-year-old Xerox veteran who had worked in corporate sales and field sales but never in manufacturing, research and development or finance. Mulcahy has no prior knowledge of money matters; how could she handle this emergency? With the connections she had made over the course of 25 years, her intimate knowledge of the company, and most importantly, her reputation as a genuine leader, she was well-suited to the position of chief executive officer. She shed blood for Xerox, and that was known to everyone. Their willingness to go above and beyond for her was a direct result of that.

Shortly after taking office, Mulcahy held one-on-one meetings with each of the top 100 executives to gauge their level of commitment to staying put in the face of upcoming difficulties. "I was aware that there were individuals who were not on my side," she stated. "Then I approached a couple of them and told them, 'This is about the company.'" Two of the individuals Mulcahy spoke with, who were in charge of large operational units, chose to quit, while the other 98 were determined to remain.

Mulcahy encouraged Xerox employees to take charge during the crisis and return the firm to its glory days. By paying off $10 billion in debt and reviving revenue growth and profitability through a mix of cost savings and innovative new products, her leadership ultimately saved Xerox from bankruptcy. The outcome was a tripling of the stock price.

Every leader, like Mulcahy, is responsible for achieving financial success. Authentic leaders can maintain their successes through good times and bad by establishing a virtuous cycle where the outcomes support their leadership effectiveness. Their ability to inspire others on their team to step up and take charge is a key component to their success, which, in turn, helps them recruit top talent and ensure that everyone is working towards the same objectives. The true test of a leader is not how well they perform temporarily, but how consistently they produce excellent results. While it's feasible to achieve immediate success without being genuine, we've found that genuine leadership is the surest path to enduring success in the long run.

Unique benefits are bestowed upon genuine leaders. The satisfaction of guiding a group of people to success in completing a noble mission surpasses that of any personal accomplishment. No amount of anguish can compare to the relief that comes from crossing the finish line alongside your loved one. It is supplanted by an overwhelming sense of contentment at having empowered people and improved the world. For genuine leaders, that is both the test and the reward.

11

The Differences Between the Best CEOs and the Average Ones

We are all familiar with the cliché that great CEOs are outgoing characters. They are advertising themselves. They are willing to take chances. However, are these generalizations accurate? What characteristics genuinely set chief executive officers apart from other executives? And, most importantly, what characteristics distinguish successful CEOs from other CEOs in the same position?

When it comes to chief executive officers and the qualities that characterize their level of success, there is a tremendous lot of speculation and legend. Thus, what qualities should businesses search for in a new chief executive officer?

This question has never been more relevant than it is in today's quickly changing marketplaces, where digital disruption is hovering over every organization. There has been a research endeavour that has been directed by Russell Reynolds Associates in collaboration with Hogan Assessment Systems. The goal of this research is to distinguish between myth and reality by identifying critical leadership indicators that have a quantitative impact on the growth of a firm. Traditional characteristics such as extroversion or self-promotion are not as strongly associated to best-in-class CEO leadership as the results reveal that intensity, the capacity to prioritize and focus on substance, and the ability to know what one does not know (and utilize the best in what others do know) are more strongly related to these characteristics.

Due to the fact that we utilized Russell Reynolds Associates' and Hogan's unique psychometric databases as the foundation of the study, we believe that our data-based approach is particularly pertinent. Researchers from other institutions have investigated these topics regarding chief executive officers by conducting interviews, examining resumes and even analysing speech patterns. We chose an in-depth approach, creating detailed psychometric profiles of 200 global CEOs, using the results of three well-established psychometric instruments: the Sixteen Personality Factor Questionnaire (16PF), which provides an overall measure of adult personality, including interpersonal skills, emotional factors, resiliency and communication style; the Occupational Personality Questionnaire (OPQ-32), which measures management and leadership style and behaviour, including how people try to influence others, their approaches to innovative thinking and self-motivation; and the Hogan Development Survey, which measures areas for development or potential derailing factors in managers and executives, including their decision-making style and independence of thinking. We corroborated the tendencies that we found in another worldwide sample of 700 CEOs that was developed by our partners at Hogan. After that, we compared these CEOs to the non-CEO executives that were contained in our proprietary database of 9,000 senior leaders.

Across a wide range of personality characteristics, our research showed that chief executive officers (CEOs) are significantly different from the rest of the executive community. There are two characteristics that stand out in particular: the ability to take risks that are appropriate and a tendency to prioritize taking action and making the most of possibilities. These characteristics are what we know to be the 'essence' of the personality of the CEO. To put it another way, in comparison to other senior executives, a chief executive officer is substantially less cautious and more willing to take action upon occasions.

Regarding the preconceived notions, although we did find that chief executive officers, in general, are more likely to be risk takers than other executives, we did not discover that they are consistently extroverted or self-promoting.

Furthermore, there are six other characteristics that distinguish the average chief executive officer from other CEOs on a statistically meaningful basis:

- the ability to be a catalyst for others to take action
- the ability to be driven and resilient
- the ability to think creatively
- the capacity to envision the future
- the ability to develop teams
- the ability to communicate effectively

It is extremely uncommon to have access to such comprehensive psychometric data concerning the thought of the CEO. Even more uncommon is the ability to find a connection between psychometric data and the performance of a company. In order to establish that connection, we developed a quantitative barrier consisting of a compound annual growth rate of five per cent during the tenure of the CEO.

When we compared the outcomes of the CEOs who performed the best to those of their counterparts who were less successful, we discovered that the CEOs who performed the best in their class stood out in three different ways:

- Not only do they have a stronger sense of purpose and mission, but they also exhibit passion and a sense of urgency. Frequently, these characteristics are exhibited in the form of intensity, impatience and a great sense of ownership and immersion in activities. Additionally, they are characterized by a strong desire to move forward. Not so long ago, researchers at McKinsey released related observations concerning newly appointed chief executive officers. In a nutshell, they proposed that the worst thing that new chief executive officers can do is "sit on their hands." "The most successful chief executive officers are those who move boldly and quickly to transform their companies." When it comes to making decisions and doing actions, we do not support judgements and actions that are excessively spontaneous or impulsive. However, we do value efficiency and speed in conducting analyses and when executing on strategy.

- They value substance and getting to the heart of the matter. The ability to go beyond the specifics and comprehend the bigger picture and the context is something that they possess. When it comes to how they think and behave, they have a strong sense of priorities. The ability to "separate the signal from the noise" is exactly what we mean when we talk about this. The most effective chief executive officers have a "nose" for identifying the most significant problems, difficulties, dangers and opportunities that an organization is now facing. Their perspectives on prioritization are crystal clear and frequently extremely independent, despite the fact that they draw from a wide variety of inputs and debates. In light of the fact that retail is becoming increasingly multichannel, online, digital and global, chief executive officers (CEOs) need to be thinking about customer demand fluidity, globalization,

- regulations and exchange-rate volatility, to name just a few of the concerns that retail CEOs are juggling.
- Rather than concentrating on oneself, they are more concerned with the organization, the outcomes and results, and other participants. They are able to maintain an open mind, actively seek out further information, and actively learn. They are one of those people who "know what they don't know." The concept of a CEO who is somewhat humble is one that many people find to be contradictory. Meanwhile, a significant amount of literature has been done on the subject of the benefits that humility can provide to chief executive officers. Our findings provide evidence that the Level 5 CEOs described in Jim Collins's book *Good to Great*—leaders who are 'a study in duality: modest and willful, shy and fearless'—can be associated to desirable organizational results. This proof is based on facts. Warren Buffett is a fantastic illustration of how this collection of characteristics can manifest themselves in a leader: Buffett estimates that he spends 80 per cent of his day learning in an effort to have a better understanding of businesses, markets and prospects. This is despite the fact that he is in charge of what could be regarded one of the most successful organizations that has ever been established. We summarize, of course, that outstanding CEOs need to be able to act boldly in tough and uncertain situations; they need to be able to create and convey a strong point of view; and they absolutely need to be extremely determined. The extra point that needs to be made here is that the most effective chief executive officers (CEOs) need to have the belief that the greatest idea prevails, and that they

frequently receive the best ideas based largely on how they work with others using a collaborative approach.

When it comes to successful chief executives, there is no one profile that fits all. In each and every instance, boards will be required to evaluate a comprehensive range of business situations prior to deciding their desired composition. A genuine extrovert, or someone who is eager to brag about the company's achievements through a variety of social gatherings that occur on a regular basis, may be required by certain businesses. Some people might benefit from a more subdued approach, from a leader who is able to cultivate relationships without coming across as overly "salesy," and who is able to avoid causing relevant markets to become agitated. However, the ability to take risks that are both effective and acceptable, as well as the ability to seize chances in high-stakes scenarios, particularly in circumstances where the "right" response is not immediately apparent, should always be at the top of the list. It is these distinguishing characteristics that set chief executive officers apart from other top executives.

Interviewing and evaluating candidates for intensity and impatience, finding those who focus on core issues and searching for a leader who is able to have a point of view while still being open-minded and recognizing the power of the organization around him or her are all things that a board should do when they want to increase their chances of hiring a successful director. These characteristics of our best-in-class CEOs will be beneficial to almost every business because they are clear markers for the ability to act quickly, draw conclusions that are not obvious and nonlinear, connect thoughtfully across a wide variety of channels and take advantage of digital and market disruption, all of which are essential in today's dynamic markets.

Get Out of Your Comfort Zone If You Want to Be a Leader

Many individuals have viewpoints on various matters. Commentators abound in the media, making suggestions and ostentatiously advising government authorities and corporate executives on what they should do. We criticize the actions or inactions of others, as well as our bosses, during social gatherings like dinner parties and cocktail parties, as well as at work, informally, around the water cooler.

As employees, we are sometimes asked to provide our opinions on matters from a narrow, functional or departmental vantage point. On the other hand, we might provide our viewpoint before giving our employer a chance to think it through and evaluate all of the relevant factors and interests before making a major choice. This might be due to a lack of availability of other resources or, more likely, a mistaken belief that expanding our horizons isn't required of us in this role.

Although this style of expressing one's perspective could be sufficient in many contexts, it is not leadership. It takes a lot more to be a leader. The first step is to think like an owner for a moment and figure out what you think should be done from a more holistic viewpoint.

I Felt Like I Did a Solid Job

I was contacted by Jim, a consumer goods company's VP, regarding an issue he was encountering. He called to ask for my opinion because he was one of my previous students. He was still trying to process the shocking event that had just occurred.

An essential new product for Jim's company has been ready to market for some time. Under the leadership of the senior VP of a pivotal division within the organization, he was an integral part of a multi-functional launch team. The group's mission was to plan the launch, packaging, advertising and distribution of the new product from start to finish. The senior executives of Jim's company were in dire need of new growth opportunities, and the market share of multiple main goods was declining, thus this product was crucial. They naively believed that by satisfying a pressing demand in the market, this new product would restore the company's standing with buyers.

The new product and its introduction were divided up amongst the project team members. It was Jim's job to make sure the product was promoted at the point of sale. Even though he didn't think this was the most important task, he saw it as a great chance due to the project's significance and the excellent calibre of his teammates.

The product's location and display in various retail settings, including supermarkets, pharmacies and others, were meticulously planned out by him after several weeks of labour. Furthermore, he came up with alternate POS materials that would be utilized in next regional product tests.

At these weekly meetings, everyone on the project team reported on what they had been working on. The senior vice president wanted everyone on the team to know what was going on with the launch in every way. He was hoping that by asking each other questions and finding out what everyone was responsible for, the team could come up with a better launch plan.

At first, Jim was proud of his accomplishments on this endeavour. "I felt I performed an excellent job," he informed me. Several of Jim's subordinates were part of the workgroup that came up with the specific strategy. What followed was rather unsettling because he was pleased with how things were progressing.

Jim had the opportunity to share his final recommendations during one of the project team meetings in the late stages. A number of team members unexpectedly and harshly panned his plan. According to them, it didn't make sense given the product's characteristics, price range and expected customer behaviour. In instance, the bigger team thought his point-of-sale positioning lent itself more to impulse buys, while they were adamant that the product should be priced and positioned as more of a deliberate purchase.

The news jolted Jim. He was pulled aside by the team leader after the meeting and asked to clarify his understanding of the newly introduced product. In response, Jim stated, "I've been in every meeting and I've listened carefully." The team leader wanted to know how he could be so different from the rest of the team when it came to the product's positioning if that was the case. In response, Jim said that he felt he had done a good job of taking notes during meetings and using what he had learned from previous successful launches.

"Who do you believe should purchase this product?" was the first of several pointed questions posed by the team leader to Jim. What is the best way to price it? Which packaging would you recommend? Since these matters weren't directly related to his job description for this project, Jim confessed that he hadn't given them much consideration. He maintained that the concerns should have been shared amongst the other team members.

Infuriating the team leader, Jim spoke his mind. He offered Jim some sage advise before the meeting came to a close. Instead of viewing himself as an individual with a limited role on the team, he encouraged him to consider how he would respond to these inquiries in his role as team leader.

This suggestion seemed strange to Jim. Inquiring about my thoughts on the situation and seeking advice on how to address the project manager's difficulty, he contacted me by phone. "Jim, your team leader has provided you with some excellent advice," was my simple response. And I concur with him. Act as if you're the one to blame for this mess. Put yourself in the shoes of the boss or even the owner of the company for a while. Let your mind wander to a time when your very survival hinged on the flawless execution of this launch. What is your recommended approach? You have a lot of talent, man. Put yourself in the shoes of the owner and respond to his inquiries with your skills.

Since neither his present nor his former employers had ever pushed him to think or behave in this manner, Jim admitted he hadn't considered this strategy. He admitted that he would need to do some deep introspection and analysis before tackling the task.

"Indeed," I replied. "You certainly do if you aspire to leadership.'

He made up his mind to give this challenge his best. He consulted with his colleagues on the team and used his extensive set of abilities to consider all facets of the product's positioning. He went so far as to do his own study at certain stores to observe the product positioning of competitors. Upon reflection, he came to the realization that his earlier suggestions were, at best, superficial, and, at worst, completely at odds with his current vision for the product launch.

A disturbing realization hit him: he had performed a terrible job. When working on this project, he had not adopted a leadership mentality. Consequently, he had brought shame upon himself and the organization with his shoddy job. He mustered up the bravery to express his apologies to the project manager and his colleagues.

His apologies were well-received by the project team. His courage in admitting he was mistaken, returning to his work and reconsidering his recommendations was admirable. His teammates were immediately on board once he explained the new placement suggestions. Returning to the team made him feel like he belonged again.

It dawned on him that he had picked up some useful information from this ordeal. "From this point forward, Jim, I hope you'll act like a leader in this company," the senior vice president informed him, reinforcing this. The vice president was a rising star in the company. You need to adopt an owner mentality if you want to realize your full potential here. Give a wide, rather than a specific, description of your work.

Instead of behaving like a restricted functionary, Jim vowed to himself that going forward he would treat his job like he was the owner of the company. Because of this shift of perspective, he was able to think more clearly and accomplish more in his career. He could now evaluate his thoughts and deeds through a fresh lens.

Establishing Faith

"Think like an owner." How easy that sounds. Indeed, it is not an easy task. You have to imagine what it's like to be the decision-maker. After a while, you might decide you'd rather not be in that situation. Everything is very complicated, with too many factors to think about and too many people with vested interests. Dammit, it's not my job! It's tempting to think narrowly in light of the complexity, constancy of change, and abundance of problems in today's environment.

As a leader, it is your responsibility to do so. You should try to accept and even welcome the feelings of frustration, agony or increased tension that it elicits from you. You will become better at this as you do it more often. Thinking like an owner is crucial to your effectiveness in your career, and I strongly suggest that you start believing and internalising this idea. To reach conviction, one must think like an owner. The word "conviction" is used to define the point at when one feels extremely certain in acting according to one's deepest beliefs.

The pursuit of absolute certainty regarding one's course of action in any given circumstance is a lifelong pursuit for many leaders. The truth is that they might not always have a firm stance. Until they attain a certain level of certainty, they continue to collect data, suffer and evaluate.

On the flip side, leaders shouldn't jump to conclusions or be so set in their ways that they miss out on important factors that could make or break their decision-making. We are all susceptible to ideological viewpoints, have blind spots and may not even be conscious of our own small prejudices. So, it's important for all of us to take our time, think about other perspectives, feel our feelings and make sure we're coming to a fair decision.

What I mean is that looking for a conviction can be a tough process. Things like the nature of the context, the behaviours of competitors, the degree to which a product becomes a commodity and so on are always evolving. Furthermore, several individuals may arrive at different conclusions regarding the best course of action when presented with the identical scenario. Leaders need to analyse, consult with others, discuss potential solutions and ruminate in order to deal with all of these factors. You can feel like you're grinding through this process most of the time.

You don't have to have all the answers or even know what to do all the time while you're grinding away at this. But as a leader, you should always aim to be completely convinced on important matters. Tell me the process. It is critical that you and your group concentrate on the processes that will lead you to a reasonable conclusion.

As you gain experience, you will have a deeper understanding of who you are and how to live by your convictions. The more you look for it, the more adept you will get at focusing your efforts to achieve that state of mind. Leaders don't waste time finding reasons they can't take charge. Rather, they rise to the challenge of ownership and inspire their colleagues to follow suit.

12

Chief Executive Officer Thoughts: What Great Leaders Do First and Best

When the idea of emotional intelligence in the workplace started to gain traction, we often overheard executives saying, "That's incredible," and then adding, "Well, I've known that all along." This was in response to our research showing a clear correlation between an executive's financial success and emotional maturity, as demonstrated by traits like self-awareness and empathy. The study's main point is that emotionally intelligent people, or "good guys," come out on top.

We expect the same response from the two years of fresh research that we have just assembled. First they'll say, "No way!" and then they'll add, "But of course!" Our research shows that the leader's attitude and actions have the most startling impact on financial results. Together, they were a domino effect, with the leader's demeanour and actions influencing those of the followers. A toxic workplace full of pessimistic, opportunity-ignoring underachievers is the product of a cruel and irritable boss, while a positive and welcoming leader produces followers who are up to any task. Profit or loss is the last rung on the ladder, which is performance.

In no way does our finding about the outsized influence of a leader's "emotional style," as we term it, diverge significantly from our investigations into EQ. Nevertheless, it does provide a more in-depth examination of our previous claim that the emotional intelligence of a leader shapes a specific work environment or culture. We found that environments characterized by high emotional intelligence promote learning, trust, healthy risk-taking and information sharing. Anxiety and terror permeate environments where emotional intelligence is low. Organizations may see short-term success when workers are anxious or fearful, but this will never be sustainable.

One of the goals of our study was to trace the path that emotional intelligence takes from top management all the way to financial success. "How is the chain held together?" we inquired. We looked to the most recent findings in neuroscience and psychology to address that topic. In addition to the data provided by the Hay Group on the leadership styles of thousands of CEOs, our own experience working with company leaders and the insights shared by colleagues regarding hundreds of leaders were also considered. We learned from this corpus of literature that emotional intelligence is like electricity: it flows through a company like a network of wires. More specifically, the leader's attitude is genuinely infectious, and it permeates the entire company like wildfire.

Let's shift our focus to the important consequences of our finding before we delve into the science of mood contagion. Emotional leadership would be the leader's top priority, if his or her attitude and actions were such powerful factors in determining the success of a company. Not only should a leader maintain a positive, genuine and energetic attitude on a regular basis, but he should also make sure that his followers do the same by modelling these traits himself. The leader's inner life must be managed in order for the correct emotional and behavioural chain reaction to take place in order for financial results to be managed.

Naturally, keeping one's inner life under control is no picnic. It is the greatest obstacle that many of us must overcome. It might be as challenging to precisely gauge the impact of one's emotions on those around them. An example of this is a CEO we know who insisted everyone viewed him as positive and dependable, but whose subordinates told us they thought his optimism was forced and even false, and that he was unpredictable with his decisions. This widespread discord is known as "CEO disease." The takeaway is that authentic leadership requires more than just a facade. An executive must exercise self-reflection to learn how his emotional leadership affects the team's attitude and performance, and then he must be equally self-disciplined to change his conduct as needed.

That doesn't mean leaders can't have poor days or weeks; life isn't perfect. Positive emotions can be genuine, positive and grounded in reality; our research does not imply that they need to be overly exaggerated or constant. To be sure, leaders have a lot on their plates, but it doesn't mean they can ignore the consequences of their own emotions and actions. This chapter presents a method for CEOs to gauge the influence of their leadership on others and offers suggestions for how to fine-tune that assessment. Before we get into CEO sickness, let's examine why it's uncommon to talk about moods at work, how the brain makes moods contagious and why this is important to know.

Absolutely Not! Sure Thing

Our earlier prediction that "No way" would be the most common reaction to our new discovery was not in jest. Even in leadership and performance literature, the topic of a leader's emotional influence is rarely addressed. "Mood" is too subjective for the majority of individuals. The United States of America is both the most legally bound and the most shockingly frank nation when it comes to personal concerns (just watch the *Jerry Springer Show* and similar shows). The age of a job candidate is not even a question we may ask. Therefore, it could be seen as an invasion of privacy to discuss an executive's emotional state or the emotions he induces in his staff.

Because it is, to be honest, a delicate subject, we may also shy away from discussing the effects of a leader's emotional style. How long has it been since you included a subordinate's emotional state in a performance review? Although you might have made passing references to your mood, such as saying, "Your work is hindered by an often negative perspective" or "Your enthusiasm is terrific," it's improbable that you actually addressed your mood or how it affects the organization's performance.

But there will also be many who say "but of course" in response to our study. Because we've all been on the receiving end of an enthusiastic manager's encouragement or the receiving end of a demoralizing boss's criticism, we all know that a leader's emotional state significantly impacts performance. The former put a positive spin on things, which led to the realization of ambitious objectives, the defeat of rivals and the acquisition of new clients. The second one made labour quite difficult. Other departments in the company turned into "the enemy," employees started to distrust one another and clients started to disappear as a result of the boss's gloomy demeanour.

Both our own and other social scientists' findings corroborate the authenticity of these accounts. There are too many studies to list them all here, but taken together they demonstrate that followers perceive things in a more positive light when their leader is smiling. As a result, they become more positive about accomplishing their objectives, more creative and better at making decisions and more likely to be helpful to others. For instance, a 1999 study by Alice Isen at Cornell University indicated that people's ability to take in and process information, apply decision rules to complicated judgements and think creatively is enhanced in an energetic setting. Mood and financial success have been directly linked in other studies. For example, in 1986, researchers from the University of Pennsylvania's Martin Seligman and Peter Schulman showed that insurance agents with a more optimistic view were more successful in closing sales because they were able to persevere through rejections more easily.

Those Evil Managers Who Succeed

Everybody has heard of that boss who is both aggressive and unpleasant, who seems to lack emotional intelligence but manages to get the company ahead nonetheless. What gives rise to those nasty, yet incredibly successful, if the emotional state of a leader is so crucial?

We should examine them more closely first. A high-profile executive may not always be the one driving the company's direction. Division heads report directly to the CEO of a conglomerate and are responsible for leading employees and influencing profits, even though the CEO may not have any followers at all.

Additionally, it is worth noting that there are instances where a SOB boss possesses admirable qualities that mitigate his negative conduct; yet, these qualities may go unrecognized by the business media. When he first arrived at General Electric, Jack Welch showed a firm hand as he led a dramatic turnaround for the corporation. It was the right moment for Welch to use his authoritative, command-and-control approach. Little attention was given to Welch's subsequent transition to a more emotionally intelligent style of leadership, particularly when he reframed the company's purpose and rallied his employees to support it.

Putting those disclaimers to one side, let's return to the notorious corporate executives who, despite their ruthless leadership styles, seem to have produced excellent financial outcomes. For instance, critics point to Bill Gates as an example of a boss who gets away with a tough approach, even if it could conceivably hurt his business.

A different light is cast on Gates's allegedly detrimental behaviours by our leadership model, which demonstrates the efficacy of particular leadership styles in specific contexts. (The *Harvard Business Review* article "Leadership That Gets Results," which published in the March—April 2000 issue, explains our model in depth.) Gates is the consummate achievement-driven leader in an organization that has recruited exceptionally gifted and determined individuals. When people are skilled, motivated and require little direction—qualities shared by Microsoft's engineers—his seemingly harsh leadership style—baldly challenging them to surpass their past performance—can be highly effective.

To sum up, a naysayer need only point to a "rough and tough" boss who got the job done in spite of his poor behaviour to cast doubt on the value of leaders who control their emotions. Our position is that there are instances where a leader is a good fit for a particular company. However, jerkish leaders should generally change their ways or face the consequences of their behaviour.

Over time, many executives lose their jobs because their emotional leadership styles lead to a dysfunctional workplace. (Although, disappointing outcomes are more often than not given as the cause.) Nevertheless, things need not come to that conclusion. A leader's inability to manage their own emotions can have a negative impact on their followers, yet a poor mood can also be lifted. You can see the how and the why by taking a look inside the brain.

Emotional Research

An increasing amount of brain research indicates that leaders' moods impact the emotions of others around them, whether positively or negatively. The scientific community has identified this as a result of the emotional brain region known as the limbic system's "open-loop" characteristic. Whereas open-loop systems rely on outside forces for regulation, closed-loop systems are able to control themselves. That is to say, our social ties are the primary determinants of our emotional states. An evolutionary success, the open-loop limbic system allowed humans to emotionally support one another, allowing a mother to calm her wailing baby.

Thousands of years after its inception, the open-loop design remains unchanged in its function. Intensive care unit studies have demonstrated, for instance, that having a sympathetic companion reduces a patient's blood pressure and delays the production of artery-clogging fatty acids. Another study indicated that middle-aged men who experience social isolation are three times more likely to die than men who have numerous close relationships. Intense stress can be defined as three or more occurrences of severe financial difficulties, a loss of a job or a divorce.

In what is formally known as "interpersonal limbic regulation," one individual can influence another's hormone levels, heart rate, sleep cycle and immune system via the transmission of signals. This is how partners in a relationship can induce feelings of warmth and tenderness by stimulating the release of the feel-good hormone oxytocin in one another's brains. However, our physiologies mix in every facet of social life. Because of its open-loop architecture, our limbic system allows others to influence our physiological state and, by extension, our emotions.

We seldom give the process of the open loop any thought, despite its pervasiveness in our lives. By monitoring physiological variables like heart rate during a pleasant discussion, scientists have managed to capture the emotional attunement in a controlled environment. Both of their bodies are moving at separate speeds when the contact starts. However, following the initial 15 minutes, their physiological profiles begin to resemble one another.

When people are in close proximity to one another, their emotions tend to spread uncontrollably, as researchers have observed time and time again. Even nonverbal expressions can have an impact on others, according to research by psychologists Howard Friedman and Ronald Riggio from 1981. Take the case of three strangers who sit silently facing each other for a minute or two. The most emotionally expressive person in the group will subtly convey their mood to the other two.

Group members will always "catch" one other's emotions, whether they're in a boardroom, an office or a factory. Moods, both positive and negative, were divulged within two hours of a meeting in a 2000 study by Caroline Bartel of New York University and Richard Saavedra of the University of Michigan. The study included seventy work teams from different industries. Researchers found that teams of accountants and nurses watched each other's moods over the course of several weeks, and that this tracking was mostly unaffected by the common problems experienced by the teams. So, just like people, groups experience a wide range of emotions, from envy to sadness to joy. Humour, when used appropriately, can lift anyone's spirits.

When You Smile, the Entire World Does, Too

You know that old cliche, right? It's quite close to the mark. While we have demonstrated that mood contagion does occur in the brain, we have also shown that not all emotions are equally contagious. Sigal Barsade of Yale School of Management found in 1999 that, in the workplace, positivity and warmth spread like wildfire, whereas negative emotions like anger and sadness were the slowest to catch on.

The fact that laughter is the most infectious feeling ever should not be surprising. When we hear someone laughing, it's nearly hard for us to control our own chuckle or smile. That's because when we see a grin or a chuckle, our brains have certain open-loop circuits that trigger an automatic reaction. Our ability to form bonds through shared experiences, such as laughter and smiles, may have been encoded into our brains long ago, according to scientists.

Humour speeds up the development of a happy atmosphere, which is the most important thing for leaders who are tasked with controlling their own and others' moods. Humour, like the leader's overall demeanour, needs to mesh with the reality and culture of the organization. Genuine laughing and smiles, we would argue, are the only ones that spread.

Everyone is watching the boss, therefore the first mood to rise tends to rise the quickest. To read his emotional clues, they look to him. When a boss isn't in the spotlight, like a CEO who works in a private office on a higher floor, his demeanour still has an impact on his subordinates, which in turn causes a domino effect to spread across the organization.

See That CEO as a Physician

If the leader's disposition is crucial, then it's in their best interest to be in a good mood, isn't it? Indeed, however, there is more nuance to the complete response than that. When a leader is enthusiastic, their mood has the biggest influence on performance. Still, it needs to be in sync with those in his immediate vicinity. Dynamic resonance is what we mean by this.

Quite a few executives, we discovered, are clueless about whether or not they resonate with their teams. Instead, they have CEO illness, which manifests itself in the form of the afflicted person's complete lack of awareness of how his or her demeanour and behaviour are seen by the organization. The majority of leaders do care about their reputation. However, they naively believe that they are capable of deciphering this data on their own. Even worse, they believe that someone will inform them if they are negatively impacting someone. It's not true.

"I feel like I'm not getting the truth so often," according to one CEO in our study. The fact that no one is ever being completely honest with me makes it so I can never pinpoint it. However, I have the impression that certain people are trying to conceal facts or information. No, they aren't being completely forthright, but they are also withholding important information from me. Doubt is a constant companion of mine.

There are a lot of reasons why followers aren't fully forthcoming with leaders on the emotional toll they've taken. Being the bearer of bad news can be terrifying, especially when there's a chance of being shot. Some people think it's inappropriate to offer commentary on such a sensitive subject. Some people aren't aware that they want to discuss the consequences of the leader's emotional style, but that sounds too general. For whatever reason, the CEO can't count on his followers to voluntarily provide him with all the information he needs.

Assessing the Situation

Our method for discovering oneself and reinventing oneself is not as novel nor as derived from popular psychology as many of the self-help programmes given to executives nowadays. The three lines of inquiry that formed its basis instead focus on the most directly related aspects of emotional intelligence to good leadership and how CEOs may hone these skills. We started using this data set to build the five-step method in 1989, and since then, thousands of CEOs have benefited from it.

Our method is grounded in brain science, unlike conventional coaching. Just like eye colour and skin tone are not encoded into a person's DNA, neither are their emotional talents, which include their attitude and abilities towards life and work. They are so ingrained in our neurology that, in some respects, they could as well be.

Indeed, there is a hereditary component to an individual's emotional intelligence. Take shyness as an example; it's not a mood in and of itself, but it might cause a person to be unusually reserved, which could be interpreted as a "down" mood, according to scientists. People in general seem to be abnormally upbeat until you meet their parents, who are themselves unusually joyful. It has been my experience that I have always been happy, as one CEO puts it. Although it irritates some individuals, I am not easily irritated. Even after his divorce, my brother was able to look on the bright side of life.

Although there is a hereditary component to emotional intelligence, environmental factors significantly influence gene expression. Even though they were born into joy, a child who loses both parents or is physically abused may develop depression as an adult. Finding a satisfying hobby can transform a grumpy child into a happy adult. However, by the time we reach our mid-20s, our emotional skill sets are mostly fixed, and the behaviours that go along with them have become deeply ingrained habits, according to the research. The catch is that our brain circuitry gets hardwired in such a way that we will continue to feel and act in accordance with our previous patterns of behaviour, regardless of whether we are joyful, depressed or irritable.

It's for this reason that leaders must possess high levels of emotional intelligence. Emotionally intelligent leaders are self-aware, regulate their emotions well, are empathetic, and know how to improve the moods of others around them through relationship management.

The goal of this five-step procedure is to teach the brain to act in a way that is more in tune with emotions. First, you must accept your actual self as other people see you. Then, you must envision your ideal self. After then, put those plans into action in order to close the gap between your ideal and actual lives. The last step is to assemble a support system of loved ones and coworkers who will act as change enforcers and ensure the process continues. Let's take a closer look at the procedures.

"Just Who Am I Aiming to Be?"

As a senior manager in the telecom industry in northern Europe, Sofia was aware that she needed to reflect on the impact of her emotional leadership style on others around her. Reading management books, working with mentors, and attending leadership seminars had not altered her patterns of poor communication and taking over subordinates' work when she was upset.

We had Sofia describe a typical day and envisage herself as an effective leader eight years from now when she came to us. She would be doing what? This is what we inquired about. She lives somewhere, right? Exactly who would show up? Tell me what it's like. We pleaded with her to think about the things that meant the most to her and to share how her aspirations and principles informed her daily actions.

In her mind, Sofia ran a small, close-knit business with a team of ten. Her connections with her kid were open and honest, and she enjoyed trustworthy friendships and interactions at work. To everyone around her, she seemed to exude an air of effortless confidence, both as a parent and leader.

To put it simply, Sofia lacked self-awareness; when she was having problems at home or in the office, she rarely knew why. "Nothing is working right." She finally understood where her emotional style was lacking after doing this exercise, which made her imagine how her life might be different if things were going according to plan. She realized how her actions affected those around her.

"What Do I Think I Am Now?"

Step two of self-discovery is developing an objective perspective on your leadership style. This poses risks and is challenging. Challenged because few would get the courage to reveal his true nature to a superior or coworker. That kind of knowledge might hurt or even paralyse people, therefore it's risky. A healthy dose of self-delusion can be beneficial: ego-defense systems aren't necessarily negative. Optimism in one's future is more common among high-functioning individuals, according to research by Martin Seligman. In reality, their idealistic perspectives provide the impetus for the excitement and drive that may accomplish the remarkable and the unexpected. Such delusions are what playwright Henrik Ibsen referred to as "vital lies," reassuring falsehoods that we allow ourselves to believe in order to confront a frightening world.

However, it's important to moderate the amount of self-delusion. Executives should always be on the lookout for the truth, even if it will likely be watered down when they hear it. Having a completely open mind towards criticism is one approach to discovering the truth. Another strategy is to actively seek out criticism and maybe even recruit a friend or two to act as your sceptics.

Also, make sure to ask your superiors, peers and subordinates for their thoughts and opinions. Studies conducted by Richard Beatty of Rutgers University and Glenn McEvoy of Utah State University found that feedback from peers and subordinates is the most reliable indicator of a leader's performance two, four and even seven years from now.

Obviously, 360-degree feedback doesn't have someone rate your emotional state, behaviour, or the results of your efforts. The way people perceive you is, nonetheless, revealed by it. People are actually reporting their perceptions of how well you listen when they give you a listening skill rating. In a similar vein, when asking for rates of coaching success through 360-degree feedback, the responses reveal how well individuals feel you comprehend and value them. For example, if your openness to new ideas score is low in the comments, it could indicate that people find you difficult to get in touch with or don't think you're approachable. Looking for 360-degree feedback will tell you all you need to know about your emotional impact.

On this second stage, one final thing should be noted. Naturally, you must recognize your own shortcomings. However, it's depressing to dwell on your flaws alone. Knowing your strengths is crucial, if not more so, for this reason. The motivation to go on to the next stage, which is to bridge the gaps, will come from realising where your ideal self overlaps with your actual self.

"How Can I Go from This Place to That One?"

After you've compared your ideal self to others' perceptions of you, you may move on to the next step: making a strategy. This meant that Sofia needed to make preparations to increase her degree of self-awareness. So, she instituted a system wherein her coworkers could anonymously and formally assess her mood, performance and impact on others once a week. In addition, she resolved to do three challenging but doable things: write in a notebook for an hour every day about her actions, enrol in a college course on group dynamics and seek out the informal coaching of a reliable coworker.

Take Juan, a marketing executive for a big integrated energy company's Latin American branch, as an example. Think about how he did this step. The position required Juan to be a mentor, a visionary and to have an encouraging, optimistic attitude, as he was tasked with expanding the company's reach in Venezuela and the entire region. Still, Juan came out as bossy and self-absorbed in the 360-degree feedback survey. His subordinates often thought of him as a grouch, someone who was difficult to get along with even when he was being nice.

Juan was able to devise a strategy with doable improvements when he identified this gap. In order to improve his teaching style, he committed to a number of activities that would help him practise empathy, which he knew was an important talent. For example, Juan resolved to learn more about his subordinates since, in his mind, he would be better equipped to assist them in accomplishing their objectives if he had a deeper grasp of who they were. He arranged for private meetings with all of the workers so that they could open up to one another about their emotions away from the office.

Outside of work, Juan sought out opportunities to fill in the gaps in his resume, such as coaching his daughter's football team and volunteering at a community centre. He was able to test out new behaviours and see how well he understood people through each of these activities.

Here we go again, examining the brain science in action. Without realising it, Juan's attitude towards work had taken root over time, and he was attempting to break free of ingrained behaviours. The first step in changing them was making them aware of them. Situations that occurred while he was paying closer attention, such as listening to a coworker, coaching football or speaking on the phone with someone who was upset, all served as signals that encouraged him to change his behaviour and try new approaches.

Not only are these cues for habit change perceptual, but they are also neurological. A study conducted by researchers from Carnegie Mellon University and the University of Pittsburgh demonstrated that the prefrontal cortex, which is responsible for initiating action, is activated when we mentally prepare for a task. We perform better when our past activation is higher.

When we want to replace a bad habit with a good one, it's crucial to mentally prepare for it. When one is getting ready to break a habit, the prefrontal cortex lights up, according to research by neuroscientist Cameron Carter of the University of Pittsburgh. The alert prefrontal cortex indicates that the brain is paying attention to what is going to happen. In the absence of that stimulation, people tend to fall back into old, unsavoury habits: a boss who refuses to listen will sever ties with his subordinate again, a brutal boss will launch into another critical attack and the list goes on. For that reason, it is crucial to have a learning agenda. There is no way we can think creatively enough to make a difference without one.

"I Don't Know How to Make a Lasting Impression."

Basically, it takes practice to make a change last. Once again, the brain is responsible. Breaking old brain habits requires repeated doing and redoing. In order to achieve implicit learning, a leader must practise a new behaviour until it is second nature. In that case, the new wiring will take the place of the old.

As Juan found out, sometimes all it takes is visualising the desired behaviour change to make it happen. Consider the executive Tom, who aspired to become more like his ideal self—a visionary and coach—and whose actual self, as seen by his coworkers and subordinates, was cold and hard pushing.

Instead of slamming the door in his employees' faces whenever he felt they were wrong, Tom planned to learn to take a step back and coach them. Tom also started to use his commute as a time to plan out his responses to potential situations. Tom mentally went over a best-case scenario one morning on the way to breakfast with an employee who appeared to be botching a job. Before attempting a solution, he made sure he had a thorough understanding of the situation by listening and asking questions. He practised techniques to deal with his expected feelings of impatience.

Neuroscientific research confirms the usefulness of Tom's visualization method, showing that engaging in detailed mental imagery activates the same brain regions as performing the actual task. Even just mentally repeating the sequence seems to put the newly formed brain circuitry through its paces, reinforcing connections. So, let's picture some possible outcomes to help us overcome the worries of trying out more daring leadership styles.

In doing so, we can prepare ourselves to feel more comfortable when we put our new abilities to use.

In order for real change to take place, we need to create the synaptic connections in our brains. This can be achieved by mental rehearsal, experimenting with new behaviours and taking advantage of opportunities both at work and outside of it to practise them. Still, innovation and ingenuity aren't enough to bring about long-term transformation. We could use some assistance from our buddies, as the song suggests.

"I Need Assistance. Who Can Provide It to Me?"

Establishing a network of backers is the fifth stage of discovering and reinventing oneself. Consider the managers who, as part of their training for senior roles, established study groups. They initially got together to plan their professional futures and figure out how to take the lead. Before they knew it, they were talking about more than just their jobs and personal lives—their aspirations and educational objectives were now up for discussion. As they worked to improve their leadership skills, they grew to trust one another and relied on one other for honest criticism. When this occurs, the company experiences improved performance. These days, it's not uncommon for professionals to form associations like this—and with good cause. When we lead others we trust, we are able to safely experiment with new skills and techniques.

We need the support of others if we want to develop our emotional intelligence and alter our approach to leadership. Not only do we rely on other people to provide a safe space for us to experiment, but we also practise with them. We must evaluate our development as learners and obtain insight into the impact of our activities on others around us.

In fact, ironically, we rely on people at every stage of self-directed learning, from developing and honing our ideal selves to comparing them to reality and finally, to the assessment that validates our progress. The very framework that allows us to understand our progress and the value of what we're learning is provided by our connections.

Subjectivity vs Mood

We surely do not intend to imply that mood is the only thing that matters when we state that primitive leadership entails controlling your own and your followers' moods. Everything you do, from your attitude to your deeds, must be in harmony with the organization's values and the truth, as we've already mentioned. We also recognize that leaders have a lot of additional obstacles to overcome, such as those associated with strategy, recruiting and developing new products. After a long day, it's all worth it.

The message conveyed by studies in the fields of neuroscience, psychology and organizational science is shockingly clear when considered collectively. A company's performance can be sparked by emotional leadership, which can either lead to a raging success or a desolate landscape. So much depends on one's mood.

13

The Compassionate CEO: How to Hold Your Team Accountable with Empathy

Compassion and accountability have long been two aspects that leaders have been expected to strike a balance between, but in recent years, we have witnessed the pendulum swinging excessively in both sides. During the early years of the epidemic, many companies made their employees a priority by providing them with a variety of support options, including flexible work schedules, benefits for mental health and other assistance to assist them in coping with the stress of the situation. Over the past several months, as both interest rates and inflation have increased, we have witnessed leaders making adjustments to their policies. They have reduced certain benefits, encouraged employees to return to the workplace and placed a greater emphasis on results, such as meeting deadlines, achieving targets and increasing revenues.

As a result of this circumstance, employees, managers and executives are left wondering: Is it possible to establish accountability without resorting to the use of whiplash, in a manner that gives people the impression that their requirements are still being taken into consideration? The question of whether caring or results should be prioritized is a binary one. And what are the most efficient methods for establishing accountability at every level of an organization with regard to its employees?

The Art and Science of Being Accountable

It turns out that people have two different ways of perceiving accountability, and the type of accountability that leaders develop will determine the level of performance that their teams achieve.

Creating a culture of threat and blame is an example of punitive accountability, which is the type of accountability that the majority of leaders normally think of and practise. Punitive accountability involves reprimanding individuals for mistakes and failures.

Accountability that is regarded as a worthy challenge regards taking ownership of a work as an opportunity for progress and sees mistakes as opportunities to better both of these elements.

In light of the fact that there is now substantial evidence demonstrating that supporting a growth mindset improves individual performance, learning and adaptation and general well-being, leaders should seek to achieve the second type of responsibility. There are knock-on effects for the culture of the team as a result of growth-oriented accountability, which rewards people for taking chances and develops a growth mentality through its implementation. In particular, it forces individuals to discover solutions to the errors that have been committed by others, rather than pointing the finger of blame or shame at them.

Because it is a "opt-in" method, viewing accountability as a worthy challenge is empowering because it is a challenge at all. The second sort of accountability allows individuals to choose whether or not they will be accountable, in contrast to the punitive accountability that holds individuals accountable. Employees have a greater sense of personal investment in tackling significant challenges when they are able to perceive that there are benefits to learning and growing while taking ownership of their job.

Four Practices That Help You Become More Accountable

At the heart of our investigation has been the identification of the mental muscles, or the processes that are taking on within the minds of individuals while they are engaging in the practice of accountability that does not involve punishment. These muscles manifest themselves as three unique but interconnected habits: contemplating the future, taking responsibility for your commitments and focusing on finding answers.

By putting these routines into practice, individuals are able to get better results. When leaders engage in these behaviours, they are able to establish more precise expectations, anticipate a variety of outcomes and maintain the appropriate mindset among their team members, allowing them to concentrate on improving rather than on being perfect.

"Prepare Yourself in Advance"

When leaders are able to mentally imagine what is likely to occur when they delegate a task or instruction to another individual, they are able to develop a mental image of the assignment and communicate it in a manner that assures that everyone understands it. This is the essence of accountability. When a leader is able to paint a more detailed picture for themselves of how they would like the job to be done and what challenges the individual may face, it will be much simpler for them to convey that vision to the employee.

For instance, a vice president of sales would inform a junior salesman well in advance of a significant pitch meeting that the client has a tendency to interrupt and ask a great deal of questions. Instructing the salesperson to come prepared to answer these inquiries is the vice president's instruction. There is a possibility that they will even act out the scenario in order to provide the vice president with guidance on how to get back on script when they are under pressure.

It is possible that a leader who is less concerned with results will be less hands-on, working under the assumption that the employee's skills will enable them to successfully close the deal. Nevertheless, by planning ahead, the leader is able to visualize how the scenario might play out, foresee potential hurdles and raise the likelihood of success for their employees in accordance with a strategy that has been set.

It is possible for leaders to assist their employees in developing a mental image of what success looks like by having them go through this activity. The prefrontal cortex (PFC), which is a huge section of the brain located directly below the forehead and is responsible for important executive tasks, as well as other regions of the brain that are responsible for processing our senses, emotions and memories, will be activated more strongly as a result of this. When leaders are able to communicate their objectives more clearly, it will be much simpler for employees to translate those intentions into actions that follow.

The difficulty lies in comprehending the viewpoint of another individual, including an understanding of the questions they might have, the hurdles they might face and the specific strengths and difficulties that they themselves possess. In the process of perspective taking, it has been shown that there are several pitfalls, one of which is that we frequently end up inadvertently projecting our own perspective onto other individuals. On the other hand, we are of the opinion that people may significantly improve their capacity to plan ahead if they are provided with the appropriate context and a little bit of training. This is true for both leaders who are assigning tasks and individuals who are accepting them.

"Take Responsibility for Your Promises"

Following through on commitments is the second habit of accountability individuals should develop. We are of the opinion that taking responsibility for one's commitments is a skill that can be acquired, as well as one that is unintentionally acquired from other people. Someone who is meticulous about carrying out their commitments, whether they are huge or small, has the potential to become someone whom others have a great deal of faith in. This is because we unconsciously keep track of those individuals who keep their promises and those who do not. Such trust has a significant influence on the ability of all individuals to work together effectively.

The misaligned expectations can register as a threat, sapping employees' motivation through a decline in dopamine levels. However, when employees are directed to perform one thing and witness their superiors doing another, the mismatched expectations might register as a threat. It is necessary for the brain to devote valuable energy away from concentrating on important tasks in order to process the error that was in violation of our expectations. Commitments that are not fulfilled typically result in new expectations of the leader that are lower.

Take for example a situation in which a leader establishes a strict deadline for the team in relation to a large department-wide project, but the team is unable to reach the date for their segment of the job. The leader runs the danger of generating a fairness threat, which could force employees to avoid future deadlines and withdraw from crucial tasks. This is in addition to the fact that they are lowering their own expectations for they themselves. If, on the other hand, the leader had taken responsibility for their obligations, they would have prioritized their tasks ahead of time and completed their deadlines, so reaffirming to their team the significance of maintaining accountability.

"Focus on Finding Solutions"

To conclude, accountability is all about personal development. Whenever the stakes are great, it is inevitable that failures will occur. It is of the utmost importance that leaders react to those shortcomings with an impetus towards learning rather than punishment. Taking this approach is a defining characteristic of a development mindset, and it necessitates the existence of a psychologically secure environment that encourages individuals to express their mistakes.

Imagine for a moment that someone makes a mistake that results in incorrect product sales figures. In order to promote punitive accountability, a leader may choose to place responsibility on the individual who committed the mistake and then require them to labour through the night in order to correct the fault. On the other hand, this may cause members of the team to begin pointing the finger at one another out of fear of being "held accountable."

The goal of responsibility that does not involve punishment is to instill a sense of grace in these situations. As a result of the fact that everyone makes mistakes, everyone has a vested interest in correcting them and then improving the following time around. Using the preceding illustration as an example, a leader who engages in this kind of responsibility may gather the team together and inquire, "What actions will move the project forward?" It is possible that other people will offer to work an additional hour in order to assist the team in meeting the deadline.

Letting go of blame and working towards making things better is what it means to anchor on ways to solve problems. It entails conducting in-depth debriefings on both successes and setbacks, as well as continuously looking for innovative approaches to problem-solving rather than focusing on the reasons for failure. Anchoring on solutions is a talent that can be learned and is greatly influenced by the actions of those around us. This is similar to the concept of taking responsibility for your commitments. As a result, those in positions of authority should make it a point to concentrate on the path forward rather than on determining who is to blame for the situation.

"Converging When It Comes to Performance and Accountability"

When it comes to performance, accountability may appear to be a pejorative term, as if results and collegiality are incompatible with one another. However, leaders in cultures that are healthy are clear about what they expect from their team and the role that they play in the process of achieving those expectations. They visualize the ways in which things could go wrong and devise strategies to overcome those challenges. In addition, they direct the team's attention towards the results rather than the consequences for errors.

As a result of each member of the team feeling safe and secure about their position within the group, teams that engage in these practices are better equipped to be firm and truthful with one another on the subject of communication. To put it another way, there is less pressure to maintain a culture of niceness because every person has faith in their own value.

When leaders develop the appropriate routines, such as looking ahead, taking responsibility for their commitments and focusing on solutions, they will discover that the balancing act of accountability takes into account the requirements of each individual while still guaranteeing that the task is completed.

14

The Post-Pandemic CEO

One pattern that has been developing over the course of the past ten years has been amplified by the pandemic. As the world has become more digital and complicated, the range of decisions that leaders are required to make has expanded. These decisions range from strategic thinking about the big picture to cautious execution, as well as advancing technology roadmaps, upskilling personnel and engaging them in their work. And decision-making criteria have also grown, with a rising emphasis on environmental, social and governance (ESG) issues in addition to profit expectations that are more tightly defined. Because of the exceptionally intense nature of the past year, leaders have been forced to make judgements for which they have no prior expertise, and they have to do it in a short amount of time.

The leaders of today need to acquire new skills and talents in order to be successful in this new era of value generation. Our in-depth research of more than a dozen companies that have transformed and positioned themselves for success in this new world provides evidence that the leaders of these companies sought to be proficient across a wide set of characteristics rather than relying solely on their areas of strengths. These companies include Microsoft, the Cleveland Clinic and Philips, among others. They learnt how to work together with people who come from different backgrounds and have different ways of thinking, and they placed an emphasis on working together to run their firm despite the fact that they were all different from one another. You may discover additional information about the leadership poll that is being conducted at the conclusion of this post if you are interested in taking part in doing so.

According to the six paradoxes of leadership that are discussed in Blair Sheppard's most recent book, *Ten Years to Midnight*, the characteristics that the leaders that we interviewed felt to be the most significant in this new era are in good alignment with those attributes.

Chief Executor of Strategy

It is essential for leaders who wish to achieve success in this intricate and fast-paced business environment to have a clear understanding of what the new world will look like and what their company's place will be in that world. In order to accomplish this, the firm needs to have executives that are highly strategic and visionary. These individuals should be able to take a step back from the day-to-day operations and see where the world is headed. They should also be able to comprehend how value may be created in the future in ways that are different from the techniques that are used today.

Being a skilled strategist, on the other hand, is not sufficient. All leaders need to have the same level of expertise in implementation. They have to take responsibility for the transformation of the company that is required to go to the future. They must be able to translate strategy into particular measures that can be carried out, and they must be able to see that execution through to its conclusion. It is necessary for them to have the ability to make quickly operational decisions that contribute to the delivery of the road to the future.

The digital model of value creation may, in many respects, call for even more robust execution abilities than in the past. This is due to the fact that there is a great deal of work to be done in order to push the boundaries of what is feasible.

The Humble Hero

People who are willing to make courageous decisions (such as leaving certain company positions or staking out new ones) in times of uncertainty are the kind of hero leaders that are required in the digital era.

At the same time, leaders need to have the humility to admit what they do not know and to bring on board people who may have skill sets, histories and talents that are very different from their own. It is necessary for them to be open to gaining knowledge from others who may have less history in leadership roles but possess more pertinent views. Not only do they need to be extremely receptive to new technologies, but they also need to be excellent listeners in order to comprehend new methods of accomplishing things that are distinct from the ways in which they had previously done things.

Humanist That is Well-versed in Technology

In the past, executives might have been able to get away with delegating the company's technological difficulties to their Chief Information Officer or Chief Digital Officer. However, this strategy will no longer be effective. Because technology is a vital facilitator for practically everything that a company does, including innovation, product management, operations, sales, customer service, finance and any other area. Every leader needs to have an understanding of what technology can do for the organization and how it can do it.

However, in addition to this, they must have the ability to comprehend and care for individuals. They have a responsibility to comprehend the ways in which technology influences the lives of individuals, and they must assist their people in adjusting to and embracing the numerous changes that will be imposed by technology. To do this, it is necessary to engage individuals with a significant amount of empathy and honesty, thereby assisting them in accepting the changes and taking ownership of the transition.

Reputable Pioneer in the Field

In a world that is always changing and experiencing various disruptions, the mission and values of a company are perhaps more vital than they have ever been compared to current times.

In times of uncertainty, having a clear understanding of one's mission and values may be of great assistance to organizations as they navigate their way towards the production of value and relevance. At the same time that executives are reimagining the place that their company holds in the world, they must also be specific and anchored in their understanding of who they are as a firm. In order to determine how they will uniquely produce value in a manner that engages others in their ecosystems and is relevant in the future, they need to have a clear understanding of the organization's reason for being, which includes its purpose and values.

At the same time, leaders are required to experiment with new ideas and innovate at a rate that is faster than at any other moment in history. They must have the bravery to fail, and they must also be willing to embrace the failure of others. All of this experimentation and innovation, on the other hand, must not be unrestricted; rather, it must take place within the boundaries that are in line with the primary objective of the organization.

Politician with Very High Integrity

It is vital for a leader to possess the ability to garner support, negotiate, develop coalitions and partnerships, and overcome resistance in order to be successful in an ecosystem environment. In this world, organizations, institutions and individuals must work together in order to produce value.

A leader must be willing to make concessions, be adaptable in terms of making adjustments to their strategy and take one step back in order to be able to take two leaps forward. On the other hand, in order for this mode of operation to be successful, it is necessary for leaders to develop trust and integrity as the foundation of all their acts. All of the stakeholders engaged in an ecosystem must be able to trust one another in order for there to be effective collaboration within the ecosystem. Customers are only willing to give privileged insights and engage in ecosystems when they have the ability to trust how their data is handled and how they are treated.

And maintaining integrity will be essential in order to successfully manage the growing regulatory scrutiny that many businesses are likely to face. Both honesty and trustworthiness are necessary requirements for the basis of an economy that is driven by data. Due to the fact that these are values that cannot be generated by a computer, it is necessary for human leaders to make deliberate decisions that are evaluated based on their language and behaviour.

Localist with a Global Perspective

Because of technological advancements, many barriers and distances have been eliminated. It is now much simpler to communicate with consumers located on the opposite side of the world and to work together with people who are located miles apart.

Companies that are operating in the digital age are almost compelled to think globally, even if it is merely for the purpose of gaining access to insights and talent in order to meet the requirements of local communities. In order to accomplish this, leaders are required to be able to think and interact on a global scale, to be open to new ways of thinking and to collaborate with individuals from all over the world.

At the same time, leaders in the digital age need to be acutely aware of the circumstances and preferences of individual consumers, as well as the local communities and ecosystems in which they operate, and they need to be able to respond to these factors. The executives of a company will undoubtedly be required to develop a mindset that is regionally mindful since customers, partners and institutions anticipate that the company will be responsive to their particular requirements.

Despite the fact that this list is by no means thorough, we believe that it serves as a solid beginning guide for navigating the era that is still to come. As a result of the digital era and the extent of the transformation that is required, it is necessary for leaders to continue to develop their talents and broaden their perspectives in order to effectively manage the complicated world in which we currently reside. We are of the opinion that the leaders who possess the qualities of humility, boldness and commitment to reinvent themselves will emerge as the most successful individuals in its digital era.

15

What's Your Style?
Finding the Right Balance

When it comes to your leadership style, finding the right balance and flexibility is essential.

There have been numerous suggestions for leadership styles to be altered in order to accommodate the requirements of a world that is always shifting and unpredictable. Some people believe that the traditional "command-and-control" management style is no longer effective, while more modern ways that are more flexible and collaborative have become the norm.

The truth, on the other hand, is more complicated than the phrase "out with the old, in with the new when it comes to today's leaders." For instance, we discovered that certain features of leadership that appeared to be out of date, such as making decisions from the top down and putting an emphasis on tactical execution, were incredibly helpful in navigating the unpredictability of the COVID-19 epidemic. Therefore, rather than settling on a model of emerging behaviours that is more static, we discovered that "seven leadership tensions" between the traditional world and the emerging world were a lot more realistic way to characterize the current status of successful leadership.

The assumption that a leader should adopt a fixed leadership style that is agnostic to the unique situation in which he or she is functioning is out of date, according to the findings of our research, which was done with more than one thousand managers from all around the world. There is no one method of leadership that can adequately address the multiplicity of issues that modern leaders are confronted with. This is true whether the method is traditional or new.

Therefore, rather than focusing on establishing a "leadership sweet spot," a leader should work on developing and expanding their "leadership sweet range." In proportion to the extent to which this range expands, the leader will attain greater effectiveness or versatility.

There are four main stages that must be completed in order to broaden the range of leadership qualities of an individual.

1. Acquire An Understanding of Yourself

Cognitive self-awareness is crucial. Developing your cognitive self-awareness is the first step in developing your leadership sweet spot. This involves becoming conscious of your own inherent talents and shortcomings, also known as your cognitive self-awareness. Having this information will allow you to establish a baseline or default range within which you are most at ease. In order to develop a greater sense of self-awareness, it is necessary to be receptive to criticism from outside sources, whether it be formal or informal. Additionally, it is necessary to pay attention to areas in which you struggle or want to avoid, and to recognize when your coworkers are not counting on you to accomplish a task or assignment.

One of the leaders with whom we collaborated observed that his coworkers had a tendency to assign him assignments that required him to "go deep" and exploit an existing idea (Miner), rather than venturing out with the team to discover new prospects (Prospector). It was only until he received direct feedback that validated his assumption that he came to the realization that in order to deliver the leadership that his team need during a period of disruption, he needed to cultivate a more expansive and inquisitive perspective.

2. Gain An Understanding of Your Surroundings

Situational awareness is essential. Leaders who are confronted with disruption need to have the ability to analyse their surroundings, taking into account the characteristics that are present and the consequences that these characteristics have for the work at hand. Sense-making and making sense of the world are both aspects of it. First and foremost, you must experience a certain circumstance in a manner that is both present and free of judgement. In the following step, you will need to determine which impulses from the surroundings are pertinent and then separate them from the noise.

An example of this would be a leader of a multinational fast-moving consumer products company who discovered that she was suffering with a number of difficult difficulties that may be improved by considering a wider range of perspectives. She realized that if she moved along the spectrum from being a teller to being more of a listener, it would boost her effectiveness as a leader. This realization came about as a result of receiving input in her yearly 360-degree feedback that she had a tendency to speak more than listen.

Interpersonal and intrapersonal awareness of one's experiences. Leaders are required to cultivate cognitive empathy, which can be defined as a knowledge of the feelings of the individuals in their immediate environment. This is a characteristic as well as a skill: It is true that some individuals are born with a greater capacity to perceive the feelings of others, but it is also possible to develop this ability via concentrated effort and consistent practice.

An example of this would be the director of multichannel marketing of a consumer products company who proposed an ambitious strategy for an upcoming campaign. However, she detected hesitation from her team, which lacked passion and appeared to postpone more than normal. In light of the fact that she had come to the realization that she was placing an excessive amount of weight on her intuition (an intuitionist), she began to gather evidence to back up her viewpoint (an analyst). As a result of the fact that some of these facts contradicted the plan that she was presenting, the campaign was ultimately subject to a number of significant revisions.

It is essential for a leader to cultivate intrapersonal awareness, which can be defined as the capacity to appropriately detect one's own emotional condition, in addition to develop interpersonal awareness. It was discovered by us that leaders who were able to perceive a powerful feeling regarding a circumstance and then listened to this feeling were making use of their intuitionist skill. In an ideal scenario, these leaders would then additionally ensure that these internal signals were cross-checked with what the appropriate data was indicating.

3. Extend Your Scope of Influence

In the event that you are fortunate, the behaviour that is most suited in a certain circumstance falls within the sweet range of your leadership abilities. Within the context of this scenario, the action is not overly complicated.

Nevertheless, if the circumstance requires you to exhibit a behaviour that is outside of your comfort zone, then the gap will need to be bridged. To accomplish this, you have three different options available to you.

Micro-behaviours should be practiced. Targeting micro-behaviours that bring you closer to your ultimate goal is a more effective strategy for changing your behaviour than making a major movement to change your behaviour. A micro-behaviour is anything that is relatively minor, and may even appear to be of little significance, but is in line with the path that you will take in the future.

The director of multichannel marketing who was described earlier was attempting to move away from being driven by her quest for perfection (Perfectionist) and towards becoming more at ease with speed (Accelerator). Therefore, she compelled herself to make decisions by a specific point in time, for example, by the end of the day, regardless of whether or not she had all of the information that was accessible to her.

4. Seek Out Exemplary People

Seek out people who can serve as examples. People who are similar to you but have different talents and who can serve as examples of the kinds of behaviours you want to cultivate and implement can frequently serve as a source of motivation for you.

A finance executive who was managing a new risk-management team for a shipping firm, for instance, received feedback that he was providing an excessive amount of precise, short-term guidance rather than presenting a long-term vision of the future (Tactician-Visionary). In response, he made it a point to aggressively seek out people (both above and below him) whom he considered to be visionaries and to acquire knowledge from the manner in which they conducted themselves.

Try to find assistance both within and outside of your team. There are occasions when attempting to bridge the gap between your default style and the reaction that is most appropriate would be inefficient in terms of the amount of time and effort that would be required. In situations like these, the most prudent course of action would be to take a look either inside or outside of your current team in order to fill the void.

As an illustration, a young risk manager working for a fintech company came to the realization that he was adept at adjusting his behaviour to accommodate the context of their rapidly shifting workplace (Adapter). His team, on the other hand, frequently found itself perplexed since they were uncertain about which 'constants' they might rely on. In light of the fact that a number of members of the team were excellent communicators about fundamental principles, he relied on them to modify all of his internal presentations in order to ensure that there was always a 'red thread' that linked with the messaging that had been delivered previously (Constant).

In the past, a set of leadership qualities that had been carefully honed was sufficient to shepherd an organization into the future. However, that time has long since passed. It has been brought to our attention by the COVID-19 epidemic that leaders who are able to adapt their strategies perform better than those who are only capable of doing a few things really well. In light of this, organizations demand leaders who are able to adapt along with the contexts in which they operate. This necessitates a continuous growth of self-awareness, situational and emotional intelligence, and behavioural experimentation in order to extend their behavioural range. Leaders are required to gather new behavioural experiences and experiment with a variety of approaches and behaviours, learning over time which ones are appropriate for a specific situation and gaining knowledge about which ones are appropriate. This is an example of a learning loop in which people perform a behaviour and then reflect on the experience to get an understanding of what went well, what did not go well, and how to improve for similar situations in the future.

16

What do the Employees Need? Being a CEO in Times of Uncertainty

Many organizations are experiencing increasing levels of volatility, and leaders are finding themselves leading within an era of overwhelming complexity. Consider the rising tendency over the long period of the World Uncertainty Index (WUI). Why do we recruit leaders in this setting? One possible answer is to look to Clayton Christensen's work-to-be-done theory.

We seek out leaders to help us navigate times of uncertainty, for one thing. We can only read about Isaiah Berlin's "well-ordered, painless, contented, self-perpetuating equilibrium" in political theory. Since the future is full of unknowns, there will always be a need for strong leaders. However, will they be sufficient?

Navigating a typical range of uncertainty, complete with its inevitable highs and lows, is one thing. However, what is the best way to lead when there are a lot of threat conditions, such as the accumulation of inflections, disruptions and dislocations in recent years? When the unpredictability threatens to cripple your team members, how do you take the helm? How can you infuse your staff with motivation and draw even more energy from the organizational system? In Longfellow's words, how can one "go forth to meet the shadowy future without fear"?

After 30 years of advising business executives in a variety of sectors, I can say with confidence that high levels of uncertainty need not lead to despair, disengagement or a drop in output. Surprisingly, I've seen numerous instances when performance improves as uncertainty increases. How is that even conceivable?

Employee engagement, morale and productivity are all aspects of the internal performance environment that a leader can significantly impact, in contrast to the external competition environment, over which they have almost no control. When faced with tremendous uncertainty, how can leaders assist their people to thrive? Even in the most trying of times, you can motivate your staff by following these four simple steps:

Develop Robust Confidence

In the face of tremendous environmental uncertainty, a reliable leader balances it out by being remarkably predictable in their own actions. I was fortunate enough to work for a Fortune 500 CEO for a long time who fostered an environment of deep trust among his staff; as a result, they could accurately anticipate his every move. He is completely predictable—in a positive way! The VP of human resources told me, "We know his values, we know his skills, so we can forecast how he will react and what he will do." A leader forms an unofficial agreement with their personnel when they consistently meet their goals. This relationship of deep trust strengthens with time.

Trustworthy leaders are the only ones capable of inspiring their followers to exert their full discretion in the face of tremendous uncertainty. What philosopher Russell Hardin dubbed a "street-level epistemology of trust" is what keeps them going: their experience in the trenches has given them insight into your character and abilities, which they can use to predict how well you will do in the future. They are able to overcome their worries and move forward with greater confidence because of your reliability.

Visual Inoculation

To envision a better future and motivate followers to work towards it is an important part of being a leader. In times of profound uncertainty, having a clear vision provides individuals with long-term motivation that goes beyond their basic survival instincts to work hard and cope with stress. You may get people to accept high levels of uncertainty as intrinsic to the process of getting to the end goal if you can articulate the organization's aim in a compelling vision. In times of trouble, your people will have something solid to rely on thanks to your vision.

Think about how the global semiconductor sector is so incredibly cyclical. A CEO I collaborated with in this field relies much on vision. He is quick to recognize and prepare for the temporary setbacks that are inevitable, and he is continually warning the company to brace itself for these disruptions. However, he also motivates the group to see past the short-term problems and focus on the bigger picture of becoming an industry leader on a global scale. Avoiding temporary setbacks is possible with a focus on the long term. That is the unspoken complexity of a well-thought-out plan, the driving force behind staying active in the face of catastrophic uncertainty. People get much-needed perspective when their field of vision is expanded.

Be Forthright and Honest

Honesty and transparency provide a third buffer against severe uncertainty. The worst kind of leadership is when the leader tries to instill unrealistic levels of confidence through empty speech. When leaders try to calm people's anxieties with empty assurances, it makes me shudder. "The market will recover in the next six months," "No one will lose their jobs," "These priorities are set in stone," "This new product will far exceed our conservative revenue forecast," and "Your team will not be affected by this," are just a few of the statements I've heard from leaders.

Extreme uncertainty impairs people's decision-making and social abilities and causes them to become threat inflexible. They fill the silence with pessimistic commentary, warped interpretations, gloomy forecasts and fatalistic scenarios; in short, they catastrophize. Have faith in your abilities and know that you can face whatever the future brings, but be careful not to make any rash promises.

View Uncertainty as a Chance for Growth

As a last tactic for leaders to employ when faced with tremendous uncertainty, try viewing it as an opportunity. Think about how organizations mainly function: to execute and to innovate. Making and delivering value in the here and now is what we call execution. For this, we rely on what are known as the "certainties" of the status quo, which encompass the present state of affairs in terms of strategy, capability and resources. Conversely, innovation is the process of making and delivering value in the future by embracing uncertainty. Something cannot be used for profit at this time simply because it is uncertain.

For this same reason, I'm employed by a chief executive officer who enthusiastically welcomes each economic crisis. In his industry, he views the dense veil of uncertainty as a chance to explore new markets, products and acquisitions. As demand declines, he patiently waits for his rivals to implement cost-cutting measures before using his strong financial position to acquire assets at a discount, with the intention of reaping the benefits of exploitation once the market improves. His new way of looking at uncertainty as an opportunity has changed how the company is run and how its people feel about it. The CEO has effectively severed the emotional connection between fear and uncertainty, replacing it with optimism, wonder and expectation. This company is stepping up its game while its rivals are taking a winter break.

A leader's capacity to instil internal stability in the midst of external turmoil is especially valuable at times of great uncertainty. The flexibility of an adaptable organization is going to be more important in an unpredictable world. Leaders must discover strategies to instill trust and stability in the face of overwhelming uncertainty. Thick trust, vision inoculation more honesty and transparency, and viewing unpredictability as an opportunity are ways they might accomplish this.

17

Staying Strong: The CEO's Guide to Resilience and Adaptability

In an era where change has become the norm rather than the exception, resilience and adaptability have emerged as the defining characteristics of effective leaders. These qualities are no longer optional but essential for CEOs who must navigate uncertainty, disruptions and the rapidly evolving business landscape. While strategic foresight and planning remain critical, the ability to withstand shocks, bounce back from adversity and pivot when necessary are what truly differentiate successful CEOs from the rest.

At its core, resilience is about enduring challenges and emerging stronger, while adaptability is the ability to change course when needed, often under immense pressure. Together, these traits form the bedrock of modern leadership, empowering CEOs to guide their organizations through turbulence, while inspiring their teams to rise to the occasion.

But what does resilience and adaptability look like in practice? And how can CEOs cultivate these traits not only in themselves but also in their organizations? This chapter explores the many facets of resilience and adaptability, drawing from real-world examples and providing actionable insights for current and aspiring leaders.

Building a Resilient Mindset

The first step toward becoming a resilient leader is developing a resilient mindset. This involves changing the way one approaches challenges, setbacks and uncertainty. It's about seeing obstacles not as threats but as opportunities for growth and learning.

Take Howard Schultz, the former CEO of Starbucks, for example. When Schultz returned to Starbucks in 2008, the company was struggling financially. Sales were declining, and customer satisfaction was at an all-time low. Rather than panicking, Schultz embraced the crisis as a chance to rethink the company's strategy. He made bold decisions, such as closing all stores for a day of retraining and refocusing the company's efforts on improving customer experience. His resilience in the face of adversity not only saved Starbucks but also positioned it for long-term success.

Resilient leaders are those who can maintain clarity and composure, even when the pressure is immense. They don't shy away from tough decisions or uncomfortable truths. Instead, they face them head-on, confident in their ability to weather the storm.

But resilience is not just about an individual leader's mindset. It's about creating a culture of resilience within the organization. A resilient organization is one that can absorb shocks, adapt to new realities and continue to thrive, no matter what challenges come its way. This requires fostering an environment where employees feel empowered to take risks, experiment and learn from failure.

Learning from Setbacks

One of the most critical aspects of resilience is the ability to learn from setbacks. In business, failure is inevitable. Even the most successful companies experience setbacks, whether it's a failed product launch, a missed opportunity or a global crisis. What sets resilient leaders apart is their ability to extract valuable lessons from these experiences and use them to inform future decisions.

Consider the example of Apple. Before becoming one of the most valuable companies in the world, Apple faced a series of challenges, including the ousting of Steve Jobs in the 1980s and a near-collapse in the mid-1990s. Yet, through these setbacks, Apple learned valuable lessons about innovation, customer experience and corporate culture. When Jobs returned to the company in 1997, he applied those lessons to transform Apple into the powerhouse it is today. His resilience, combined with his ability to adapt to changing circumstances, played a crucial role in Apple's resurgence.

CEOs must adopt a similar approach. When faced with failure, they must resist the temptation to assign blame or dwell on what went wrong. Instead, they should focus on understanding the root causes of the setback and identifying what can be learned from the experience. This process of reflection and learning is what allows leaders to turn failure into future success.

The Power of Adaptability

While resilience is about enduring and learning from adversity, adaptability is about the ability to pivot in response to changing conditions. In today's fast-paced business environment, the most successful CEOs are those who can adapt quickly and decisively to new challenges and opportunities.

A prime example of adaptability in action is the response of companies during the COVID-19 pandemic. Faced with unprecedented disruption, CEOs across industries were forced to make rapid decisions to ensure the survival of their businesses. Some companies, like Zoom, were able to capitalize on the sudden shift to remote work by quickly scaling their services to meet skyrocketing demand. Others, like restaurants and retail stores, pivoted to new business models, such as online ordering and delivery, to stay afloat during lockdowns.

CEOs like Brian Chesky of Airbnb demonstrated adaptability by shifting the company's focus during the pandemic. With travel demand plummeting, Chesky had to make difficult decisions, including laying off employees and cutting costs. However, he also used the crisis as an opportunity to rethink Airbnb's business model, focusing on long-term stays and expanding into new markets. By remaining adaptable, Chesky was able to navigate the crisis and position Airbnb for future growth.

Adaptability is not just about responding to external challenges—it's also about anticipating change and staying ahead of the curve. CEOs who are proactive in adapting to new trends, technologies and market dynamics are better positioned to lead their organizations into the future.

Leading with Agility: Balancing Stability and Flexibility

At first glance, resilience and adaptability may seem like conflicting traits. Resilience implies stability and endurance, while adaptability suggests flexibility and change. However, the most effective leaders are those who can strike a balance between these two qualities.

Leading with agility means knowing when to stand firm and when to pivot. It requires a deep understanding of the organization's core values and long-term goals, as well as the ability to recognize when those goals need to be adjusted in response to changing circumstances.

For instance, Netflix's shift from DVD rentals to streaming video is a powerful example of agile leadership. Reed Hastings, Netflix's CEO, understood that while the company's core mission of providing entertainment remained the same, the way in which that mission was fulfilled needed to evolve. By embracing streaming technology early on, Hastings was able to position Netflix as a leader in the digital entertainment space, while other companies struggled to adapt.

Agility also means being able to lead through uncertainty. In a world where change is constant, CEOs must be comfortable making decisions with incomplete information. They must be willing to experiment, take calculated risks and adjust their strategies as new information becomes available.

In the tech industry, this approach is known as "fail fast, fail often." Companies like Amazon and Google have built their success on a culture of experimentation, where failure is seen as an inevitable part of the innovation process. CEOs in these companies understand that adaptability is not just about reacting to change—it's about driving change through continuous learning and iteration.

Fostering a Culture of Resilience and Adaptability

While resilience and adaptability are important traits for CEOs, they are equally important for the organization as a whole. Building a culture that values resilience and adaptability requires intentional effort from the top down.

One way to foster this culture is by encouraging open communication and transparency. When employees feel safe to express their ideas, concerns and challenges, they are more likely to take ownership of their work and contribute to the organization's success. This openness also allows CEOs to gain valuable insights into potential risks and opportunities, enabling them to make more informed decisions.

Another key to fostering resilience and adaptability is empowering employees to take risks and learn from failure. In many organizations, failure is stigmatized, and employees are discouraged from taking bold risks. However, in a rapidly changing world, innovation requires experimentation and experimentation often leads to failure. CEOs must create an environment where failure is not only tolerated but celebrated as a learning opportunity.

Consider Google's famous "20 per cent time" policy, which allows employees to spend 20 per cent of their workweek pursuing passion projects unrelated to their core responsibilities. This policy has led to the creation of some of Google's most successful products, including Gmail and Google News. By encouraging risk-taking and experimentation, Google has built a culture of adaptability that enables it to stay at the forefront of innovation.

Leadership in the Face of Adversity: The Human Element

Leadership in times of adversity is not just about making the right decisions or pivoting business models—it's about how leaders show up for their people. The human element of leadership becomes even more critical during a crisis. Employees look to their leaders for reassurance, guidance and a sense of stability in uncertain times.

Jacinda Ardern, the prime minister of New Zealand, provides a compelling example of the power of empathetic leadership in times of crisis. During the COVID-19 pandemic, Ardern demonstrated a remarkable balance of resilience, adaptability and compassion. Her clear and empathetic communication reassured the nation, while her decisive actions helped New Zealand contain the virus more effectively than many other countries.

Similarly, CEOs must recognize the importance of empathy and emotional intelligence when leading through adversity. It's not just about making the right business decisions—it's about understanding the human impact of those decisions and providing support to employees during difficult times. Whether it's offering mental health resources, creating flexible work arrangements or simply being available to listen, the human element of leadership cannot be overlooked.

Resilience and Adaptability as a Leadership Imperative

Resilience and adaptability are no longer just desirable traits—they are essential for CEOs who want to lead their organizations through the challenges of the modern world. In an era defined by uncertainty, disruption and rapid change, CEOs must be able to withstand adversity, learn from failure and pivot when necessary.

But resilience and adaptability are not just individual traits—they are qualities that must be cultivated within the organization as a whole. By fostering a culture of openness, risk-taking and continuous learning, CEOs can empower their teams to thrive in the face of adversity and adapt to whatever the future holds.

In the end, the ability to lead with resilience and adaptability is what will separate the great CEOs from the good ones. It's what will allow them to navigate the challenges of today while positioning their organizations for success in the future.

18

Looking Ahead: The Future CEO's Path to Leadership

As we look toward the future, the role of the CEO is no longer just about managing profits or guiding strategy—it's about shaping the future of entire industries and societies. CEOs today face a unique challenge: they must steer their companies through a world that is increasingly unpredictable, complex and fast-paced.

But What Does it Mean to Lead Beyond Today's Horizon?

This question defines the modern CEO's mandate. It means not only being adaptable and quick on your feet but also thinking deeply about the long-term consequences of every decision. The CEOs of tomorrow will not be defined by how they respond to challenges but by how they anticipate and create opportunities in a world where change is the only constant.

The Tech Revolution: More Than Just Tools

In the past, CEOs were primarily concerned with operational efficiency, financial management and stakeholder relations. Today, however, the rapid pace of technological advancement has added new dimensions to leadership. Artificial intelligence (AI), machine learning and automation are no longer just buzzwords; they are reshaping industries across the globe.

For example, look at the retail sector, where companies like Amazon have revolutionized supply chains through automation and predictive analytics. AI now helps companies not only to understand their customers' buying habits but also to predict what they might want next, allowing them to stay ahead of the competition. The CEO of a traditional brick-and-mortar store must think differently about their business model. It's no longer just about sales floors and customer service; it's about integrating AI to forecast trends, personalize customer experiences and optimize inventory.

However, with great power comes great responsibility. The introduction of AI and automation raises ethical questions that future CEOs must grapple with. For instance, while automation can increase efficiency, it can also lead to significant job displacement. Elon Musk's Tesla, a leader in autonomous vehicles, has sparked debates about the future of jobs in transportation. The role of the CEO in such companies goes beyond simply implementing new technology—they must also consider the broader societal implications and how to mitigate the negative consequences for employees.

This isn't limited to high-tech companies. In agriculture, AI-driven drones are being used to monitor crops, assess weather patterns and even distribute fertilizers. A CEO in this industry must understand how to integrate these advancements while also considering the environmental and social impact on farming communities.

In short, future CEOs will need to not only understand technological innovations but also anticipate how these technologies will shape markets, employment and society at large. They will need to lead conversations on the ethical use of AI, data privacy and the balancing act between automation and human labour. Successful CEOs will be those who can marry technological efficiency with human empathy.

Human-Centered Leadership: Navigating the Emotional Landscape

While technology will undoubtedly dominate the future of work, the human element remains irreplaceable. In fact, the more technology permeates our lives, the more important it becomes for CEOs to focus on human-centered leadership. The successful leaders of tomorrow will be those who can blend technological advancements with a deep understanding of human needs and emotions.

Consider Satya Nadella, CEO of Microsoft. When Nadella took over the company, he inherited a highly competitive, aggressive corporate culture. Rather than pushing for more of the same, he focused on empathy, inclusivity and building a growth mindset. His leadership wasn't just about turning around the company's financials (though he did that successfully); it was about transforming Microsoft's culture into one that valued people, collaboration and learning. As a result, Microsoft saw unprecedented growth, with its employees feeling more connected and invested in the company's mission.

In this context, the CEO must play the role of both strategist and emotional guide. With mental health challenges on the rise—especially post-pandemic—CEOs must lead with compassion, fostering an environment where employees feel valued, safe and supported. We've seen examples in the tech world where burnout is rampant—especially in fast-paced, high-pressure environments like Silicon Valley. Companies like Google and Apple have responded by introducing mental health programs, meditation rooms and wellness initiatives to help employees manage stress.

But it's not just about implementing perks. The future CEO must be deeply attuned to their teams' emotional needs. This requires emotional intelligence—understanding when to push and when to give space, when to offer advice and when to simply listen. It's about building trust, one conversation at a time, and ensuring that employees know they are more than just resources on a spreadsheet.

One powerful example is LinkedIn's CEO, Jeff Weiner, who implemented the practice of compassionate management across the organization. He emphasized that being a great leader isn't about being the smartest person in the room or the most aggressive—it's about showing genuine care for your team and creating a culture where compassion leads to better decision-making and higher employee engagement. CEOs like Weiner are proving that human-centered leadership is not just good for people—it's good for business.

Sustainability: The New Bottom Line

A future-oriented CEO understands that sustainability is no longer a choice—it's a business imperative. As climate change becomes an undeniable reality, companies are being forced to rethink their operations from the ground up. The CEOs who will succeed in the coming decades are those who make sustainability central to their strategy, not just as an add-on or a marketing gimmick but as a core value that drives decision-making.

Look at Patagonia, a company where sustainability is not just part of the brand—it's embedded in every facet of its operations. Patagonia's CEO, Yvon Chouinard, famously told customers to "buy less" in a campaign aimed at reducing consumerism. While this might seem counterintuitive for a business leader, Chouinard's focus on environmental sustainability helped build unprecedented loyalty and trust among consumers. Patagonia's customers believe in the company's mission, and they reward the brand with their loyalty.

In contrast, we see other companies that have been slow to embrace sustainability facing backlash. Take the oil industry, where CEOs are now facing immense pressure from both investors and the public to reduce their carbon footprints. CEOs who fail to recognize the importance of transitioning to renewable energy sources will find themselves left behind, as governments, consumers and even shareholders demand more accountability.

A recent example of forward-thinking leadership comes from Unilever's CEO, Alan Jope. Jope has integrated sustainability into Unilever's long-term growth strategy, committing to reducing the company's carbon footprint by half, using 100 per cent recyclable plastics and ensuring all employees are paid a living wage. These initiatives reflect the growing trend of CEOs not just focusing on profits but understanding that long-term success depends on how well they serve society and the planet.

For future CEOs, the challenge will be to innovate and adapt without compromising the environment. They must balance short-term profitability with long-term sustainability, and this balancing act will define the CEOs who rise to the top in the coming years.

The CEO as a Global Citizen: Responsibility Beyond Profit

Increasingly, the CEO's role goes beyond the boardroom and even beyond the company itself. CEOs are becoming global figures, expected to speak out on societal issues such as racial injustice, gender inequality and human rights. In today's interconnected world, consumers and employees alike are looking to CEOs to lead with a sense of global responsibility.

Consider Tim Cook, Apple's CEO, who has taken public stances on a variety of social issues, from LGBTQ rights to immigration policies. Cook understands that Apple's influence extends far beyond technology—it has the power to shape cultural conversations and policies. By standing up for issues that matter to Apple's employees and customers, Cook has positioned the company as a leader not just in tech but in corporate responsibility.

Moreover, the COVID-19 pandemic has shown us just how interconnected our world is. The future CEO must be a global thinker, one who understands the nuances of international politics, trade and cultural differences. They must be prepared to navigate crises that transcend borders, whether it's a pandemic, an economic downturn or a natural disaster. CEOs like Mary Barra of General Motors, who had to lead through the global supply chain disruptions caused by the pandemic, are prime examples of leaders who are adept at balancing global challenges with local needs.

CEOs will also need to ensure that their companies contribute positively to the global community, not just through donations or corporate social responsibility (CSR) programs but through core business practices. The next generation of consumers cares deeply about where their products come from, how they are made and whether the companies they buy from align with their personal values. Companies that lead with a sense of global citizenship will attract not just customers but employees who are passionate about making a difference.

A Legacy of Leadership

As we draw this book to a close, it's clear that the future of leadership is dynamic, complex and full of opportunities. The CEOs of tomorrow will need to balance innovation with empathy, profitability with sustainability and strategy with purpose. They will not just be corporate leaders but global citizens, responsible for shaping a better, more equitable future.

The greatest leaders are those who leave a lasting impact, not just on their companies but on the world. As a CEO, your legacy is defined not by the profits you make but by the people you inspire, the innovations you champion and the values you uphold. In the words of former PepsiCo CEO Indra Nooyi, "Leadership is hard to define, and good leadership even harder. But if you can get people to follow you to the ends of the earth, you are a great leader."

The future belongs to those who are bold enough to embrace it with vision, integrity and heart. And that is the ultimate challenge—and opportunity—for the CEO of tomorrow.